TOFU COOKERY

TOFU COOKERY

Soups, Salads, Snacks, Main Dishes, and Desserts

Fusako Holthaus

KODANSHA INTERNATIONAL
Tokyo, New York and San Francisco

PHOTO CREDITS: Tamihisa Ejiri, Pls. 2, 4, 5, 6, 9, 10, 13, 14, 15, 16, 17, 20, 21, 23, 24, 25, 26; Makoto Shimomura, front jacket, Pls. 1, 3, 7, 8, 11, 12, 18, 19, 22, back jacket; Katsuhiko Ushiro, back flap.

Planning and editorial work by Kodansha International and INO Planning, Mayumi Hyodo, Mitsuyo Akashi, and Yoshiko Abe; layout and illustrations, Oak Inc. and Tokiyoshi Tsubouchi; picture on page 13 is reproduced from *Tofu hyakuchin*, Rinsen Shoten facsimile edition; cooperation, American Soybean Association.

Distributed in the United States by Kodansha International/USA Ltd. through Harper & Row, Publishers, Inc., 10 East 53rd Street, New York, New York 10022.
Published by Kodansha International Ltd., 12-21, Otowa 2-chome, Bunkyo-ku, Tokyo 112 and Kodansha International/USA Ltd., 10 East 53rd Street, New York, New York 10022 and 44 Montgomery Street, San Francisco, California 94104. Copyright © 1982 by Kodansha International Ltd. and INO Planning. All rights reserved. Printed in Japan.

LCC 82–80647
ISBN 0–87011–523–5
ISBN 4–7700–1023–0

First edition, 1982

Contents

Introduction

My intention in writing this book is to break free from fixed ideas about tofu. I have endeavored to treat tofu simply as a basic material for cooking and, at the same time, to make it acceptable to the American palate.

Tofu has been part of the Japanese diet for over a millennium, and today we cannot imagine a Japanese diet without tofu any more than we can one without those other soy products, miso and soy sauce. There are, consequently, a number of preconceptions related to tofu and its preparation in the Japanese mind and a tendency to hesitate to add to or change the customary ways of eating or cooking it.

In 1979 there was a television documentary in Japan on Japanese food in North America; this documentary contained the surprising report that Americans were starting to make and eat tofu. The Japanese are well known for absorbing culture from foreign countries, but the people today also tend to believe that Japanese culture is not easily understood by foreigners. Personally, I felt some doubt on hearing this television report and was uncomfortable about how Americans might make and cook tofu. Yet, as a result of this report, all kinds of recipes for tofu dishes—Western, Chinese, and Japanese—started to appear in ladies' magazines and television cooking programs. Having become rather conservative, especially about cooking, I ignored them. I said "No" to tofu dressing, "No" to tofu quiche, and all the rest and decided that I should keep the traditional flavors rather than use tofu in such ways. I had a great attachment to and respect for traditional cooking, and it was a long time before I allowed myself to experiment with any new methods of preparing tofu.

As a housewife and a teacher of Western cookery in Japan, I have long been concerned with the Japanese diet. My husband is American, and because of his work I have lived both in America and in Southeast Asia.

My curiosity has led me to study the diets of all the countries we have visited. The life of my family—an American married to a Japanese and our children—is constant cultural exchange, a commingling of the Japanese qualities in myself with the strong American spirit of my husband; and the place where all the historical, social, ethnic, and religious ideas have risen up in confrontation or in harmony has been the dining table.

When I think back to the days of my childhood, the first thing that comes to mind is a small, clean tofu shop that was always washed down with water. There was a huge, fresh slab of bean curd in a tiled water tank. The proprietor used to cut this neatly into pieces with a wide blade in his rough, red hands. And I remember the delicious smell that drifted into the street when he fried *abura-age*.

Every morning and evening, a man on a bicycle came selling tofu from door to door, blowing on a little brass horn to announce his presence. Until quite recently, men were still selling it in this way, and I can still recall the squeal of the bicycle brakes and the sound of the lid of the wooden box full of tofu as it opened. Early in the mornings I used to hear from my bed the sounds of my mother cutting tofu for miso soup. This was done in an unvarying manner: for miso soup, it was cut into one-centimeter squares; whereas for the evening meal's clear soup it had to be cut into three-centimeter slices. And then there was my grandmother's grilled tofu cooked with eggs. This dish had a subtle flavor and made us feel as if we lived in luxury; it was a source of great pride in the family. And my mother's green vegetable stew, which contained a little fried bean curd to add to the flavor.

In summer, merely the appearance of cold tofu in a glass bowl on the dining table, with its clean-cut surfaces under water, is enough to bring on a refreshing feeling of coolness; and in winter, tofu steaming in an earthenware pot is a warming sight. Japanese dietary sensibilities are not directed only towards the pursuit of fine tastes, but are also reflected in the seasonal variations and simple beauty of everyday dishes.

The cultural exchanges with other countries that have occurred since World War II have brought great change to the diet of the Japanese. Chinese cooking, in particular, which includes many ways of cooking tofu, reached the kitchens of ordinary Japanese families during this period. The Chinese, who are said to have first made bean curd about twelve hundred years ago, usually cook it with meat or fish and a lot of oil.

Some Japanese tofu cooking has been influenced by foreign methods, but the traditional way of preparing tofu peculiar to Japan makes the best use of tofu alone, exploiting its natural flavor. Chinese cooking on the other hand blends many flavors into a harmonious whole. There is no reason, then, why tofu cannot be used successfully in Western cuisine.

With many trials and many errors, by following my experience, instincts, and imagination, I have developed Western recipes that use tofu. Using traditional methods of cooking as a basis, I have added the special character of tofu to Western dishes, always trying to find how to enhance the overall flavor. One of my first efforts was to put tofu into a food processor. To my surprise, in an instant I got soy milk, and I was delighted to think that I would be able to make soups and cakes and all sorts of other things with it, and I felt as though half the book was completed. Immediately I used this liquid to make an oyster stew. Now, it is very important not to overcook oysters, and I was careful not to use too high a heat, but something quite unexpected happened—the liquid slowly solidified! This turned out to be a result of the coagulating agent, whose work had been undone by the processor, being reactivated by the slow heat. I really felt my lack of scientific knowledge—thus, use true soy milk for soups, not tofu that has been liquefied.

Dressings and sauces are improved by the addition of tofu, because its creaminess yields a very smooth texture. The plainness of tofu lightens the taste of hamburgers and gives them a firm texture. Quiches are easy to make with tofu; in this book, I cut tofu into cubes and fry them in butter to give an added texture to the quiche.

I garnished some "silk" tofu with fruit and added a gingery syrup. The taste was wonderful—even revolutionary! Encouraged by this, I then made several desserts and came to realize that there was much more than I thought to using tofu in Western cooking.

Tofu can be used in an endless variety of forms and combinations. Its possibilities stretch from hors d'oeuvres through main courses to desserts. Of course, the main traditions of tofu cookery in China and Japan should not be ignored. I have therefore included some typical Japanese and Chinese recipes that are appealing and easy to make.

Before embarking on the details of the recipes, I would like to point to something that is both mysterious and appealing about tofu. I have written that tofu is bland, with no dominating character of its own. But actually, in contrast with its softness, it has a kind of inherent strength, which is never diluted by cooking of any kind. I have tried cooking it with butter, with cheese, with milk and honey and herbs, but, amazingly enough, whatever is done, it never loses this special subtle flavor.

As a Japanese wife married to an American and interested in Western cookery I am very happy to have the opportunity to expand the appeal of tofu and to introduce various methods of cooking it, both new and traditional, to the Western world. All the dishes in this book have appeared on my own dining table and together represent a harmonious fusion of Western, Chinese, and Japanese cooking.

The reasons for this book are numerous. It began with my appreciation of the wonderful character of tofu and the many possibilities that exist for its preparation, especially in Western-style dishes. I also came to appreciate its value as a foodstuff in the present age—it is high in nutrition and helps one avoid obesity, arteriosclerosis, heart disease, and high blood pressure.

Before putting pen to paper, I reread the Japanese book *Tofu hyakuchin* ("One Hundred Flavors of Tofu"). Written on the subject of tofu cuisine about two hundred years ago, this book introduces not just one hundred, but as many as three hundred ways of preparing tofu. In its recipes, all kinds of seasonings are used with tofu, and I saw that the real skill of tofu cooking lies in the ability to appreciate and bring out the various qualities and subtleties of this remarkable foodstuff.

I hope that, as you begin to appreciate and use the delicacy of tofu, the recipes here will lead to a pleasant, healthful, and permanent change in your diet.

Fusako Holthaus
May, 1982

TOFU FROM ITS ORIGIN TO THE PRESENT

Tofu originated in China. Many theories exist about when it was first produced, but it is agreed that this event occurred by the eighth or ninth century A.D. The first extant text mentioning tofu is a book written at the beginning of the tenth century.

It is said that the Chinese encountered cheese, yoghurt, and other dairy products in their contacts with nomadic peoples in neighboring areas. For various historical reasons, dairy products have never become part of Chinese culinary culture. At some time, the Chinese discovered that soybeans can be processed to make a "milk," and that this "milk" can, in turn, be coagulated to form something resembling cheese. It is not inconceivable that this "milk" and "cheese" (i.e., tofu) was made in emulation of the dairy products favored by the neighboring nomadic peoples, but this theory is perhaps a bit simplistic.

In the middle of the ninth century, soy milk was brought to Japan by Japanese Buddhist monks who had been studying in China. Tofu at first was treasured almost like a jewel by the aristocracy, but with the spread of Buddhism, which forbade the consumption of meat or fish, tofu became an important temple food and source of protein for the monks. To this day, prepared in various ways, it has remained a staple food in Buddhist temples.

In the Nara period (710–794) and the Heian period (794–1185), the leaders of culture were the aristocracy and the Buddhist clergy, but in the early Kamakura period (1185–1333), this role was passed to the samurai, or warrior, class. Meanwhile, Buddhism gained much ground in Japanese society and gradually brought tofu with it to the food bowls of the common people.

After the Warring States period (1482–1573), land was recovered from the ravages of battle and farm produce increased again, along with which tofu-making methods were resumed and developed.

Then, in 1782, *Tofu hyakuchin* ("One Hundred Flavors of Tofu"), a book on tofu preparation, was published. It sold extremely well in its day and was followed by a supplementary volume and reprints. Even now, it is a useful handbook for tofu cookery, though the modern form of tofu was developed at about the end of the nineteenth century.

In olden times, tofu used to be made in the depth of winter, but with the development of methods of refrigeration and sanitation, tofu now can be manufactured throughout the year. The techniques of manufacture have also been improved; the tofu sold in supermarkets is made by mechanical mass production. The natural means of coagulation using *nigari* (bittern, the liquid remaining from salt extraction) has been superseded by the chemical calcium sulfate. Yet, despite the mass production and mass marketing of tofu, the small neighborhood tofu maker is still ubiquitous and important in Japan—there are few neighborhoods without one. The tofu shops near my home are simple and small, with unassuming signboards. They sell handmade tofu, and the only apparent difference in their methods of production from thirty or forty years ago is that the wooden coagulation and flotation tubs they once used have been replaced by plastic or stainless steel ones.

The Japanese possess the ability to adopt and adapt. They have characteristically borrowed advanced techniques from other countries, modifying them to suit the national life-style. This fundamental Japanese feature is reflected also in the wide difference between the tofus of Japan and China. The demand for this soft, easily digestible, and highly nutritious product has never ceased. Tofu thus transcends age and has outlived shogunates and eras. I see no reason why its versatility and high nutritive value should not make it a favorite throughout the world.

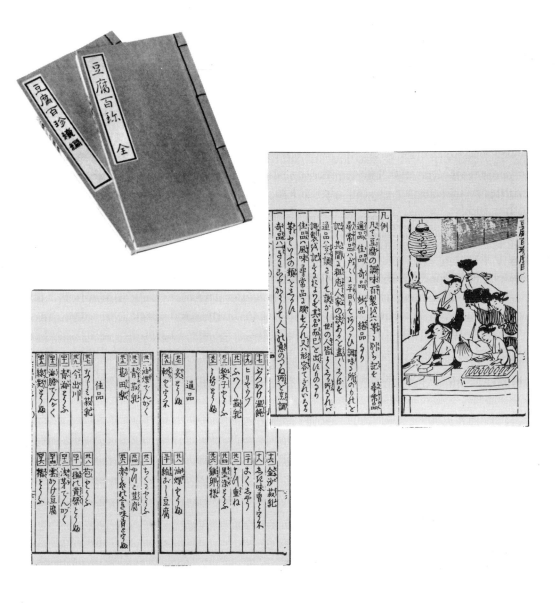

TOFU—THE IDEAL FOOD

In Japan, soybeans have long been called "the meat of the fields," and soybean-based foods prepared in a countless variety of ways are an intrinsic part of Japanese cuisine, served not only at the most elaborate imperial banquets, but also in the daily meals of ordinary people. The soybean provides complete, high-quality protein on a par with the protein found in beef or fish. It has less starch than any other bean and contains 34 percent protein and 18 percent fat, whereas red meat contains only about 20 percent protein by bulk. Moreover, soybean oil contains no cholesterol whatsoever.

The amino acids (the basic building blocks of protein) found in soybeans are of good quality. And soybean oil is composed mainly of polyunsaturated fatty acids such as linoleic and oleic acids. Among their other functions, these acids are involved in the production of lipose, a protein that apparently interferes with the build-up of cholesterol on the walls of the blood vessels. Lecithin, another substance found in abundant quantities in soybeans, has a similar function.

Tofu, a concentrated soybean product, is easily digested and contains almost all the protein found in the original bean. In fact, while eating the beans themselves provides only 71.4 percent digestible protein, tofu provides as much as 92.7 percent and is also low in calories but high in minerals and vitamins, especially B_1 and B_2. The amino acids present in tofu are not only valuable nutrients in themselves, but also aid in the digestion and utilization of many other foods.

As mentioned above, tofu is totally free of cholesterol and particularly high in linoleic acid, an essential fatty acid that cannot be synthesized by the human body. Linoleic acid has been linked to the prevention of arteriosclerosis. Tofu is an excellent food for many on restricted diets or those who wish to loose weight.

Though this book is intended for the general reader, weight-watchers and vegetarians can benefit enormously from soybean-based foods. No other food contains such an ideal balance of nutrients, is so low in calories, and so easily digested. It has been long recognized in Japan that strict vegetarians, mainly Buddist monks, are among the healthiest, long-lived members of the population. Their meatless diet contains good quantities of soybean-based foods.

THE TOFU FAMILY

Tofu is either "cotton" or "silk" tofu, depending upon the manufacturing process. These two are easily distinguished by their appearance and texture.

Other tofu family members are *abura-age* or *usu-age* (thin deep-fried tofu), *atsu-age* (thick deep-fried tofu), *ganmodoki* (deep-fried tofu "burgers"), *yaki-dofu* (grilled tofu), *yuba* (soy milk skin), and *kori-dofu* (freeze-dried tofu). In addition, soy milk (*tonyu*) and *okara* (soybean pulp) are by-products of the tofu-making process.

Each member of the family is discussed below.

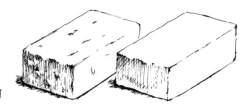

"COTTON" TOFU

This is the most common variety, and when Japanese say "tofu," this type is usually what is meant. The texture is firm and the surface is irregular.

"Cotton" tofu is produced by placing the soy milk curd in a cotton-lined container that has tiny holes. The cloth is folded over the curd, and a weighted lid is placed on the container. The weight presses out liquid and serves to make the tofu firm, and the cotton cloth leaves the impression of its weave on the surface of the tofu.

Every neighborhood in Japan has its tofu maker. The packaged tofu sold in markets is mass produced by large companies by machine and is uniform in appearance and texture. The little local tofu maker, like as not, makes his tofu by experience and not with precise or mechanical measurement of ingredients. Of course, the local tofu maker's product is much better than the packaged stuff sold in markets, yet, on rare occasions, he will make a small error. I remember once buying tofu that was too soft and later having the tofu maker's profuse apologies because he did not put enough coagulant in that day's batch. Such small surprises are a pleasure, and I hope the local tofu makers never are supplanted by the mass-produced, standardized product.

"SILK" TOFU

"Silk" tofu takes its name from its silky-smooth appearance and texture, but there are other significant differences between the "cotton" and "silk" varieties that have to do with the method of production. Unlike "cotton" tofu, "silk" tofu contains a larger amount of coagulant and has not been drained of its water. Thus, fewer nutrients are lost in the production of "silk" tofu. Silk tofu is used in recipes that take advantage of its smooth texture, but it should never be cooked at a high temperature or for a long time since it comes apart easily when heated.

I do not remember when "silk" tofu first appeared on the market. I have the impression that perhaps it is a very recent thing and that when I was younger only "cotton" tofu was sold by most tofu makers. Today, still, some tofu makers make only "cotton" tofu. Also, many tofu connoisseurs will laugh with a bit of disdain if you tell them that you use "silk" tofu for either Simmered Tofu (*yudofu*) or Chilled Tofu (*hiyayakko*). Such people claim that "cotton" is the proper tofu. Perhaps this attitude derives from the fact that the entry of "silk" tofu into the Japanese daily diet is recent.

In most of the recipes contained in this book, either kind of tofu may be used. Where I have indicated "silk" tofu, it is because its smooth texture fits the recipe somewhat better than the texture of "cotton." Delicate recipes best use the delicacy of "silk" tofu. But, you can make any recipe as delicate or robust as you like. I must stress that THERE IS NO RULE that prescribes which kind of tofu to use—whether you use "cotton" or "silk" tofu is strictly a matter of personal taste.

ABURA-AGE or USU-AGE
(thin deep-fried tofu)

Abura-age is made from tofu in which more coagulants have been used than in "cotton" tofu. This kind of tofu is cut in thin slices, press-drained under a heavy weight, and deep-fried twice. First, it is deep-fried in oil at 220° to 250°F for 2 to 3 minutes and then once again at high heat (360° to 390°F) until crisp. One cannot make this at home.

Unlike the ordinary "cotton" tofu, the tofu used for *abura-age* takes on a puffy texture when fried, and its taste depends entirely on the quality of the oil it is deep-fried in. When buying *abura-age*, look for a puffy, glossy texture and clean shape. It must be very fresh, since the oil quickly looses flavor. Before cooking, *abura-age* should be rinsed with boiling water to remove excess oil.

Abura-age is a kind of harmonizing addition in Japanese simmered foods and finds wide use in miso soups. Not too long ago it was used much more frequently than it is now. But, unlike bacon, it has not become expensive.

The fact that it can be cut across the middle and each half teased open to form a pouch into which all kinds of foods may be put makes *abura-age* marvelously convenient. For instance, fill each pouch with 1–2 Tbsps of chopped Japanese long onion or scallion and then grill the pouch on both sides until the onion is soft. A touch of miso and a slice or two of cooked carrot in addition to the onion transforms this simple idea into something different. The possibilities are endless, and any cooking method may be used.

ATSU-AGE
(thick deep-fried tofu)

Like *abura-age*, *atsu-age* is also deep-fried, but only once. It is made by first draining tofu by Method III, using a heavy weight to squeeze out as much water as possible, and then deep-frying at a very high temperature. The tofu must be of very good quality, of average thickness, and have a spongy texture.

Since quick frying at high heat cooks only the surface of the tofu, *atsu-age* keeps 2 to 3 days refrigerated.

Like *abura-age*, it should be rinsed with boiling water to remove excess oil before it is cooked. Though it is usually used in dishes that require boiling or in Chinese stir-fried dishes, it is also delicious just grilled and sprinkled with soy sauce and grated ginger.

GANMODOKI
(deep-fried tofu "burger")

The word "*ganmodoki*" means something like "imitation wild goose," because it was said to resemble the flavor of bird meat. No one ate wild goose in Japan, so this odd name is a euphemism for the fact that the flavor is somewhat meatlike.

To make *ganmodoki*, use tofu drained by Method II and pressed in a towel to remove excess water. Mash the tofu and add any chopped or sliced vegetables you like, avoiding those that are watery. In Japan a mixture of grated mountain yam, thinly sliced burdock root, carrots, seaweed, and sesame is added to the mashed tofu and mixed well. Other ingredients such as ground meat, oysters, or cooked vegetables may also be used. This mixture is formed into balls or pressed into flat patties and deep-fried twice in the same manner as *abura-age*. If made at home, *ganmodoki* may be eaten immediately, but if store bought, rinse with boiling water to remove excess oil.

In Japan a very popular *ganmodoki* dish features *ganmodoki* simmered gently in a mixture of soy sauce, saké, *mirin*, and *dashi*.

Ganmodoki must be cooked while fresh; it keeps 2 to 3 days refrigerated.

YAKI-DOFU
(grilled tofu)

Yaki-dofu is tofu that has been lightly drained and grilled. It is used in dishes that require boiling, since it does not come apart easily. Like other kinds of tofu, it should be used while fresh.

SOY MILK

Soy milk is the liquid produced when soybeans are boiled, ground, and strained. It is this soy milk that is coagulated to form tofu.

Soy milk may be used in the same manner as cow's milk. When boiled, a skin develops on its surface. This skin is *yuba* (see below), and should be removed. Raw soy milk has a peculiar flavor, which can be camouflaged by adding nutmeg or cinnamon before drinking.

OKARA

Okara is the pulp remaining after soybeans are boiled, ground, and strained to produce soy milk. It is high in protein and oil, but since it has very little flavor, it is always cooked with other, tastier ingredients.

Okara is also known by the euphemism *u-no-hana* (a type of white wild flower). Every day small trucks cart away the *okara* from neighborhood tofu makers to use as animal feed. In former years *okara* was used much more in Japanese home cooking. Another traditional use is for polishing floors and woodwork—just wrap *okara* in a cloth and apply with much elbow grease.

YUBA

When soy milk is heated, the film or skin that forms is the raw *yuba*. This may be dried; the dried form keeps indefinitely and is packaged in various forms.

The various kinds of dried yuba take their names from the shapes into which they are formed: *ita yuba* (flat yuba), *maki-yuba* (rolled yuba), *uzumaki yuba* (yuba spirals), and *toyo-yuba* (yuba "sticks"), etc. It is used in many different ways.

Yuba is not a part of Japanese home cooking. It is associated with Kyoto, where it seems to have been used in the elegant cuisine of the court aristocracy and wealthy Buddhist temples.

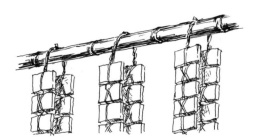

KORI-DOFU
(frozen, dried tofu)

Even when refrigerated, fresh tofu lasts only a short time, but *kori-dofu*, which is tofu that has been frozen and then dried, lasts many months.

Reconstitute frozen, dried tofu by soaking in tepid water until it becomes soft and spongy (about 5 minutes). Place in a cold-water bath and press gently between palms of hands to remove the milky liquid. Repeat this process until the water emitted is clear.

The texture of *kori-dofu* is completely different from that of ordinary tofu.

HOMEMADE TOFU

For 16 ounces (1 lb) of tofu:

2 cups dried soybeans	kitchen towel
special equipment:	thermometer
colander	flat dish to be used as a weight

Clean the beans, removing any extraneous material and moldy or discolored beans. Wash the beans and soak in water, using water equalling 3 times the volume of beans. Soak 16 to 20 hours in winter or 8 to 10 hours in summer. Soybeans will increase from 2 ½ to 3 times in size when soaked. Drain soybeans and pat dry. Measure volume of soybeans and combine with the same volume of water. Place beans and water in a blender or food processor and blend into a thick, creamy puree—about 2 minutes. This puree is called *go.*

In a large, deep pot, bring an amount of water equal to 10 times the original volume of soybeans (in this case 20 cups of water) to a boil. From this volume subtract the volume of water used with the soybeans when they were pureed. Add the *go* (soybean puree) to the boiling water and reduce to medium-low heat. Simmer for 15 minutes, stirring down to the bottom of the pot to avoid scorching. Be sure to adjust the heat carefully, because the mixture has a tendency to boil over.

Place a strainer over a deep bowl and line the inside of the strainer with a clean kitchen towel. Pour the mixture into the towel and wring out as much liquid as possible.

The filtered liquid in the bowl is soy milk; the residue in the towel is called *okara.*

Heat the soy milk in a pot at low heat (160–165°F). Dilute 1 ½ Tbsps of coagulant with ½ cup of water. Add ½ of this mixture (¼ cup) to the soy milk and stir slowly, no more than once or twice, with a wooden spatula. Wait until the temperature drops to 140°F, then pour in the remaining ¼ cup of coagulant. Again stir slowly once or twice and let simmer 2 or 3 minutes. Remove from heat.

At this point, the mixture will have separated into curds and a clean liquid, the whey. If curds still remain suspended in the liquid, stir gently and gather all loose curds together into one large curd.

Next line the colander with a clean kitchen towel. Scoop up the curd with a perforated ladle and place it in the towel-lined colander. Cover the surface of the curd with the kitchen towel and place a dish, stone, or any other heavy object about the size of a fist on top and leave for 5 to 10 minutes. The curd will gradually be pressed into the shape of the colander.

Next place the box or colander in a basin of water and remove the tofu carefully.

Soak the tofu in water for 4 to 5 hours to remove excess coagulant solution. It is now ready to eat.

Points to remember
1. Be sure to adjust the heat when simmering the *go*.
2. Be sure NOT to stir too much after adding the coagulant. Too much stirring will harden the tofu.
3. The soy milk should always be kept at 160°F. At no time should the temperature of the soy milk exceed 178°F.

Coagulant
In the past, a substance called *nigari* was used to coagulate tofu. *Nigari* is the liquid remaining after salt is extracted from sea water. Since sea water is no longer used as the source of most salt, *nigari* has become rather hard to get.

Today, calcium sulfate, available at most drug stores, is the most common coagulant. Be sure to specify high-grade calcium sulfate when purchasing. With the growing popularity of natural foods, natural *nigari* can once again be found at some health food stores.

For 2 cups of soybeans use 0.8 ounces of *nigari*, diluted in 2 cups of water. Remove about ½ cup from the top of this liquid and use it in the same way as the coagulant in the recipe.

WHAT TO DO WITH FRESH TOFU

Tofu is best when served fresh on the same day that it is made. Leftover tofu should be placed in a bowl of water big enough to allow the tofu to float freely. The bowl should be sealed with plastic wrap and placed on one of the lower shelves of the refrigerator. The water should be changed regularly, and the tofu should be eaten within 2 or 3 days of purchase.

Store-bought tofu should be allowed to soak in water. This soaking removes coagulant remaining in the tofu, and soaking for even a short time is better than not soaking at all.

The full, subtle flavor of tofu can be enjoyed best if these few pointers about how to serve and store tofu are observed.

PREPARING TOFU FOR COOKING

Tofu is prepared for cooking by eliminating some of its water content. This draining uses one or a sequence of methods, depending on the firmness required.

Method I   Wrap tofu in a clean kitchen towel and let stand for 30 minutes.

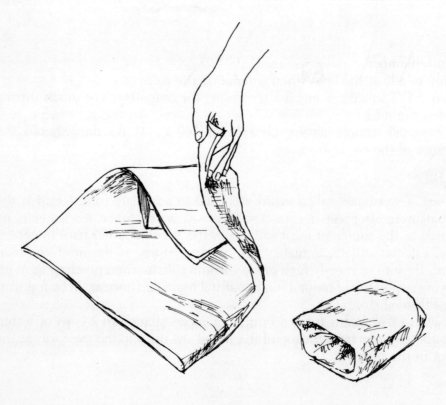

Method II Place a cutting board or cookie sheet on the *towel-wrapped* Tofu I and add weight (cans, etc.) up to about 2 pounds. Leave for another 30 minutes.

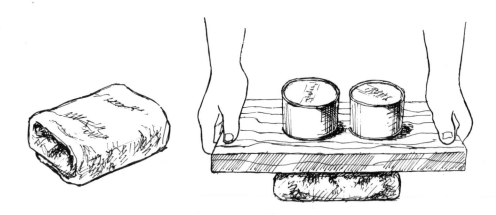

Method III Slice Tofu II as shown below, sprinkle with salt, *wrap in a clean kitchen towel,* and press as in Method II for another 30 minutes. The tofu will now be firm enough to be handled easily

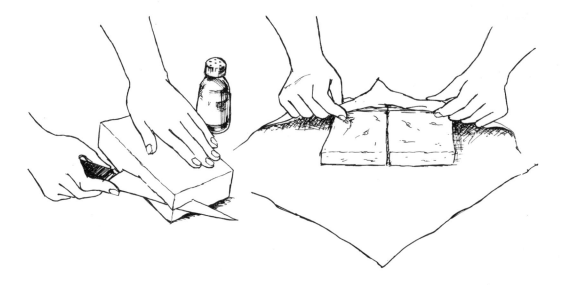

Most recipes in this book will call for tofu drained by Method I, II, or III. In some cases more water is pressed out by wrapping the tofu in cloth and gently squeezing.

Basic Recipes

Four basic recipes will be helpful to readers not familiar with Oriental cooking. I have assumed such basic Western preparations as chicken and meat stock are known to everyone. Japanese cooking uses *only short-grain rice*, whereas Chinese and other cuisines use long grain. The Japanese method of cooking rice is included because it may be unfamiliar to many readers.

DASHI (makes about 4 cups)

12×3-inch sheet *kobu* kelp	1 cup lightly packed dried
4½ cups water	bonito shavings
	(*katsuobushi*)

Wipe *kobu* well with a damp cloth. Soak the *kobu* in the water for 30 minutes to 1 hour, without cooking, then remove. (If boiled, *kobu* becomes thick, heavy, and glutinous.) Bring the water to a boil, add the bonito shavings all at once and bring to a boil again. Remove from heat and let the bonito shavings sink to the bottom. Strain. Use *kobu dashi* instead for vegetarian dishes.

KOBU DASHI (very delicate)

2 ounces *kobu*, wiped with a damp cloth	4 cups water

Let *kobu* stand in water 30 minutes. Place on low heat until just boiling. Remove *kobu* immediately before the water boils. Use this *kobu dashi* for vegetarian dishes.

CHINESE SOUP STOCK (makes about 8–10 cups)

1⅔ lbs chicken	½-inch square fresh ginger,
15 cups water	crushed
	2 scallions

Wash chicken well. Place chicken, water, and ginger in a heavy kettle or pot and bring to a boil. Reduce the heat, skim off foam, add scallions, and simmer 1½ to 2 hours. Strain broth gently through a double thickness of cheesecloth.

HOW TO COOK SHORT-GRAIN RICE

Wash the rice and let it drain in a colander for 30–60 minutes. Put it into a pot and add the same amount (volume) of water as the drained (not dry) rice. Cook over medium heat. When it boils rapidly, stir with a spoon. Cover tightly and put in a preheated 300°F oven for about 20 minutes. Remove from the oven and let it settle for 5–10 minutes. Next, fluff the rice gently with a wooden spoon and place a kitchen towel under the lid to catch moisture. The result will be a firmer rice. If you prefer softer rice, add 10 percent more water.

Plate 1   *Autumn Leaf Tofu; Tea Ceremony Tofu (pages 43, 44)*   *Deep-Fried Tofu and Cucumber (page 44)*
         Okara and Herring (page 45)   *Deep-Fried Yuba (page 47)*

Egg Rolls (page 49)

Tofu and Celery
with Sesame Dressing (page 51)

Yuba Rolls (page 51)

Spiced Tofu (page 48)

Plate 2

Steamed Fish Balls (page 47)
Chilled Tofu with Four Chinese Sauces (page 53)

Plate 3

Tofu Puffs
(page 57)
Meatballs
(page 56)
Tomato Tartlets
(page 54)
Tofu Fruit Squares
(page 54)
Onion Tartlets
(page 55)

Plate 4

Hot and Sour Soup *(page 67)*
Scallop Soup *(page 68)*
Wakame Seaweed and Ginger Soup *(page 68)*

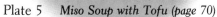

Plate 5   *Miso Soup with Tofu (page 70)*

Plate 6   *Oyster Stew (page 65)*

Plate 7

Shrimp Quenelles
au Gratin (page 78)
Veal Stew (page 82)
Beef Rolls with Tofu
Stuffing (page 73)

Plate 9   *Stir-Fried Tofu, Beef, and Tomato (page 92)*

Plate 10   *Jia-Chang Tofu (page 95)*

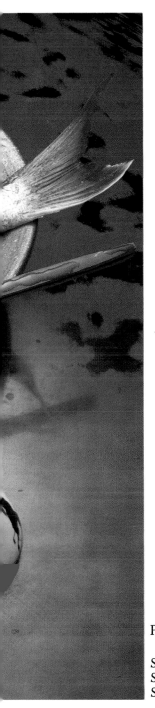

Plate 8

Steamed Sea Bream with Kenchin Filling (page 98)
Sukiyaki (page 100)
Steamed Savory Custard (page 69)

Plate 11   *Heavenly Tofu (page 97)*

Plate 12

Sautéed Tofu and Crabmeat (page 93)

Plate 13

*Chinese Deep-Fried Tofu
(page 96)*

Plate 14

Stir-Fried Green Vegetables and Tofu (page 96)

Plate 15   *Deep-Fried Tofu;*   *Scrambled Tofu (pages 103, 104)*

Plate 16

Tofu Steak (page 83)

Plate 17

Spinach Quiche (page 77)

Plate 18 *Simmering Tofu (page 102)*

Plate 19   *Chilled Tofu (page 102)*

Plate 20

*Apple and Celery Salad
(page 116)*

Plate 21   *Spring Garden Salad (page 117)*
Pao-Cai Salad (page 118)

Plate 22

*Red Cabbage and
Blue Cheese Salad
(page 111)*

Plate 23   *Pumpkin Pie; Banana Custard; Oatmeal Cookies (pages 151, 146, 141)*

Plate 24

Chinese Tofu Custard (page 154)

Plate 25

Yuba Rolls with Sweet Bean Jam (page 154)

Plate 26

okara (soybean pulp)

soy milk

frozen and dried tofu

deep-fried tofu "burgers"

fresh yuba

grilled tofu

dried yuba

"cotton" tofu

"silk" tofu

thin deep-fried tofu

thick deep-fried tofu

Hors d'Oeuvres

AUTUMN LEAF TOFU

Nishiki-Dofu   (color plate 1)

The green and red tints of autumn are seen in this baked (originally steamed) custardlike traditional dish.

(serves 4)

1 ¼ cups *dashi* (see p. 24)
2 Tbsps soy sauce
½ tsp salt
1 Tbsp sugar
¼ cup saké
1 small carrot, cut into
   julienne strips

5 large eggs
½ cake tofu, drained by
   Method I and lightly
   squeezed in cheesecloth
2–3 okra pods, sliced

Preheat oven to 350°F.

Bring *dashi*, soy sauce, salt, sugar, and saké to boil. Add carrot and cook until soft. Cool in pot liquor.

Place eggs and tofu in blender or food processor and process until smooth.

Stir in carrots, carrot pot liquor, and okra.

Pour mixture into greased 9×9×2-inch baking dish and bake 25 minutes or until a knife inserted in center of the custard comes out clean.

Cool on rack to room temperature and cut into 1-inch squares.

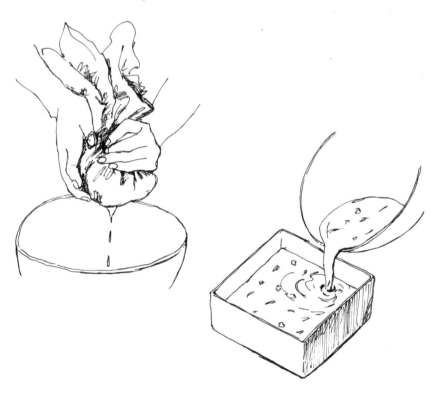

TEA CEREMONY TOFU

(color plate 1)

The traditional tea ceremony has close associations with Zen Buddhism. As a result, many of the dishes, elegantly prepared from simple and wholesome ingredients to accompany the tea ceremony, were originated by Buddhist orders and are often known by the name of the temple where they were created. In its simplicity, the taste and visual beauty of this dish typifies the essence of both Japanese cuisine and the tea ceremony. It is traditionally prepared using the special *natto* (fermented black beans) for which the Daitoku-ji temple in Kyoto is famous. If *Daitoku-ji natto* is not available, Chinese fermented black beans are very close in flavor and are a good substitute.

(serves 4)

3 cups *dashi* (see p. 24)
¹/₈ tsp salt
¹/₂ cake tofu, cut into
  1 × 1 × ¹/₂-inch cubes

¹/₄ cup *Daitoku-ji natto* (or
  Chinese fermented black
  beans or sliced black
  olives)

Heat *dashi*, salt, and tofu, uncovered, over low heat to simmering. Remove tofu, arrange on plate, and garnish with a bit of *Daitoku-ji natto*.

DEEP-FRIED TOFU AND CUCUMBER

(color plate 1)

This dish combines tofu with tenderized cucumber strips in a thick sesame seed dressing for a delicate and provocative taste sensation. With the addition of a little sugar and *miso*, the dressing recipe shown here is excellent with cooked spinach.

(serves 4)

1 cucumber, cut in half
  lengthwise, seeded, cut into 1 ¹/₂-inch lengths, and
  then into julienne strips
salt
1 sheet thin deep-fried tofu
  (*abura-age*), rinsed quickly
  with boiling water to
  remove excess oil and
  blotted dry

dressing:
2 Tbsps sesame paste
1 tsp soy sauce
¹/₄ cup *dashi* (see p. 24)
1 Tbsp saké

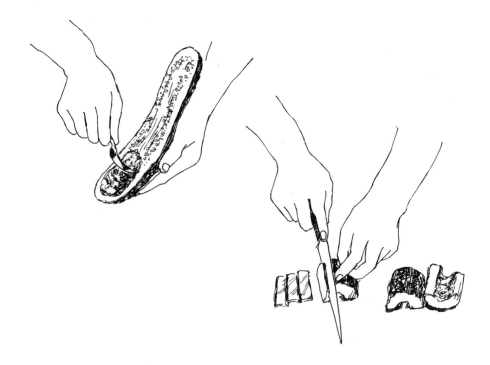

Sprinkle cucumber strips with salt and set aside for 30 minutes. Rinse off salt and squeeze out water.

Pan-broil both sides of *abura-age* in an ungreased skillet, 1 minute on each side. Remove, cut in half lengthwise, then across into julienne strips.

Mix dressing ingredients and combine with cucumber and *abura-age*.

OKARA AND HERRING

Unohana Mabushi   (color plate 1)

One of the many traditional dishes eaten at New Year in Japan, the original recipe calls for the use of *kohada*, a fish very similar to herring, though a little smaller and not quite so oily. I have found that bottled marinated herring makes a convincing substitute for *kohada*. *Okara* is the lees of tofu. It has a delicate flavor all its own and is used in many wholesome dishes. Such is the nature of tofu that its goodness can be used right to the last drop.

The first days of the New Year in Japan are traditionally a time of relaxation. Since hardly any cooking is done at this time, almost all the food for the holiday season must be prepared in advance. One of the reasons for the popularity of this dish is that, if properly prepared, not only will it keep for several days, but its flavor gets better with time. The whiteness of the *okara* sprinkled over the fish is reminiscent of the first light snowfalls of the year.

(serves 4)

dressing:
²/₃ cup *okara,* pressed
   through a sieve
1 egg white
¹/₂ tsp sugar
¹/₂ tsp salt

2 Tbsps saké

8 ounces marinated herring
   fillets (bottled; without
   sour cream)

Place dressing ingredients in the top of double-boiler and cook over low heat, stirring constantly, for about 10 minutes or until liquid is completely absorbed. Remove from heat and chill.

Slice the herring diagonally into 1-inch pieces and drain on a paper towel. Sprinkle both sides of herring with dressing and place on serving dish. Sprinkle with more dressing.

The dressing may seem dry at first, but it will absorb moisture from the herring and make a nice coating. When handling, avoid using your fingers; use a fork or chopstics—this is very fragile.

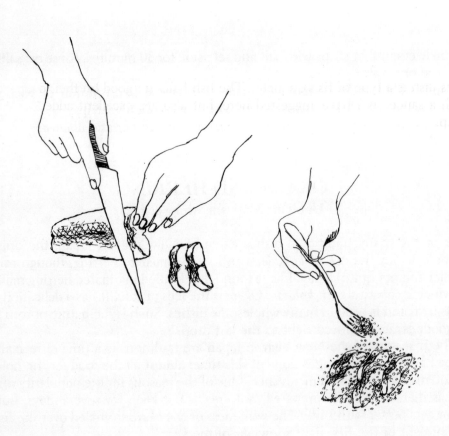

DEEP-FRIED YUBA
(color plate 1)

vegetable oil for deep-frying
dried *yuba* sheets, cut into
   quarters with scissors
salt

Heat oil to medium temperature (340°F). Add *yuba* 1 piece at a time. Work quickly; frying time is about 10 seconds. Take care not to burn. Drain on paper towel.
   Salt lightly and serve.

STEAMED FISH BALLS
(color plate 2)

This dish is a type of fish quenelle. The fish balls are good on their own, served with a sauce, as I have suggested here, but also are excellent added to a clear soup.

(serves 4)

½ lb white-fleshed fish
   (flounder, sole, etc.)
½ cake tofu, drained by
   Method I
1 egg white
1 Tbsp cornstarch
1 tsp salt
2 Tbsps saké
2 Tbsps vegetable oil or lard
⅛ tsp white pepper
black olives and/or carrots,
   cut into ⅛-inch pieces

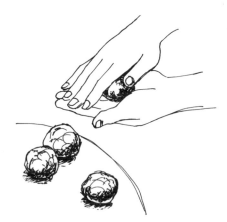

Place all ingredients except black olives and/or carrots in blender or processor and process until mixture is smooth.
   Line a steamer with a damp cloth and heat over high heat.
   Moisten hands and form fish-vegetable puree into 1-inch balls. Place in

preheated steamer and decorate with black olives and/or carrots. Steam, covered, over high heat for 15 minutes.

Serve with one of the following sauces:

sauce I
2 Tbsps soy sauce and 1 tsp finely slivered fresh ginger root

sauce II
2 Tbsps vinegar-soy sauce, catsup, and cayenne pepper to taste

sauce III
2 Tbsps soy sauce and ½–1 tsp prepared mustard

SPICED TOFU
(color plate 2)

You can buy this Chinese food packaged from most reputable Chinese food stores, but of course the flavor cannot be compared with that of the homemade variety. Spiced tofu, if properly prepared, keeps well and can be refrigerated for as long as a week without the flavor being impaired. It makes a good companion to freshly cooked rice.

(serves 4)

4 Tbsps lard or oil
½ cup saké
⅔ cup water
¼ cup soy sauce
⅛ tsp each cloves, cin-
  namon, powdered ginger,
  and cayenne

pinch sugar
1 cake tofu, drained by
  Method II, cut into
  1 × 1 × ¼-inch pieces,
  wrapped in kitchen towel,
  and drained another hour

Put all ingredients except tofu in a pot, cover, and bring to boil over medium heat. Add tofu, reduce heat to low, and simmer, covered, until the liquid is absorbed.

EGG ROLLS
(color plate 2)

The egg rolls that are an all-time favorite in Chinese cuisine usually contain a filling that includes ground pork. Here I have made them into a totally vegetarian dish by substituting tofu for the pork. It is the sauce, made either from a mixture of soy sauce and hot Chinese mustard or soy sauce and vinegar, that adds the crowning touch to this dish, so do not skimp on it.

(30 pieces)

egg roll wrappers:
2 large eggs
1/8 tsp salt
1 tsp cornstarch
vegetable oil

filling:
2 Tbsps sesame oil or lard
2 Tbsps finely chopped
　scallions or chives
1/2 lb spinach leaves, wash-
　ed, drained well, and
　chopped

1/2 tsp each salt and pepper
1/8 tsp each cloves and
　powdered ginger
1/2 cake tofu, drained by
　Method I, lightly squeez-
　ed in cheesecloth
1/4 tsp salt
1 Tbsp vegetable oil
1 egg white

flour-water paste

wrappers:
Mix eggs, salt, and cornstarch well. Lightly oil an 8-inch skillet and heat until medium-hot. Pour 1/4 of the egg mixture into heated pan and quickly tilt to cover bottom with a thin, even layer of egg mixture, as you would when making crepes. Cook over low heat 1–2 minutes; turn over and cook another 30 seconds. Remove and drain on paper towel. Repeat with remaining egg mixture, greasing pan between each wrapper. There should be 4 wrappers.

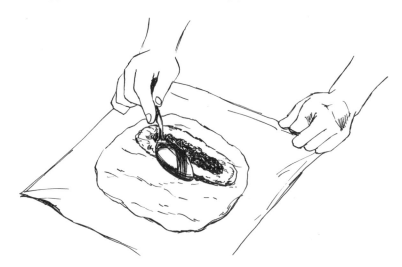

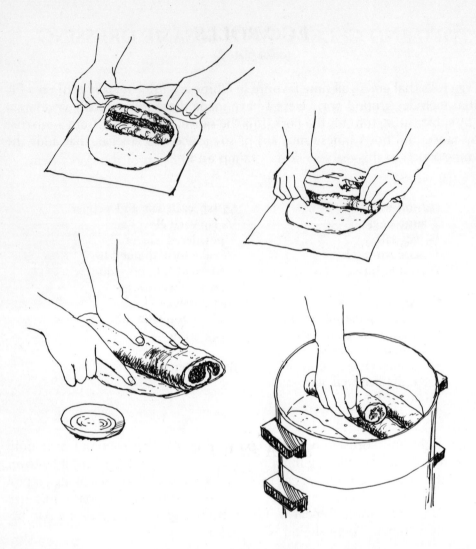

filling:
Heat sesame oil or lard in skillet and sauté scallions 1 minute. Add spinach and sauté another 3–4 minutes. Season with salt, pepper, and spices. Cool to room temperature.

Combine tofu, salt, oil, and egg white.

Place one wrapper on a cloth, spread ¼ of the tofu mixture on it, then ¼ of the spinach filling; roll, using the cloth. Moisten the end of the wrapper with flour-water paste and press firmly to seal roll.

Place the rolls in steamer with sealed side down and steam over high heat 10–15 minutes. Cool to room temperature.

Cut into ½-inch pieces and arrange on serving plate showing the attractive, colored filling.

TOFU AND CELERY WITH SESAME DRESSING

(color plate 2)

This is an hors d'oeuvre frequently served in Taiwan. The type of tofu there is not the same as Japanese; it has a "skin," and it is this that is used in the original recipe. Traditionally it was served garnished with *chin cai*, a kind of watercress. In this recipe I have substituted celery hearts, since they are quite close to *chin cai* in flavor. It is important to use only the most tender part of the celery heart.

(serves 4)

dressing:
2 Tbsps sesame oil
1 Tbsp saké
½ tsp salt
pepper to taste

¼ cup finely chopped
celery hearts

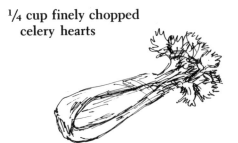

½ cake tofu, drained by
Method III and cut into
julienne strips

Combine dressing ingredients and mix with tofu and celery. Flavor improves if prepared in advance.

YUBA ROLLS

(color plate 2)

This recipe is one of my favorites. Sautéing the rolls gives them a crisp finish and brings out their flavor. They may also be steamed or deep-fried. Preparation is easy and takes hardly any time. Fried rolls make a tasty addition to dishes simmered in a soy sauce and *dashi* mixture.

(makes 30 pieces)

2 Tbsps vegetable oil
1 clove garlic, finely
chopped
1 stalk celery, finely
chopped
1 cup bean sprouts
½ cup finely chopped boiled or canned bamboo
shoots
2 lbs mustard greens, parboiled, squeezed, and
chopped

1 tsp salt
pepper to taste
1 Tbsp soy sauce
¼ cup saké
4 10-inch squares dried
yuba, sprinkled with
water to make them
pliable but not too soft
cornstarch-water paste
2 Tbsps vegetable oil

Heat oil in skillet and sauté garlic over low heat for 1 minute. Add celery, bean sprouts, bamboo shoot, and mustard greens and sauté for 8 minutes. Season with salt, pepper, soy sauce, and saké.

Cut *yuba* in half. Place ⅛ of the filling in the center lengthwise, bring up both sides, and fold into thirds. Moisten edges with cornstarch-water paste and press firmly.

Heat 2 Tbsps oil in skillet and brown *yuba* rolls on both sides.

Cut each roll into 2-inch pieces and serve as is or with dipping sauce made from soy sauce and mustard, or soy sauce and sesame oil, or soy sauce and vinegar.

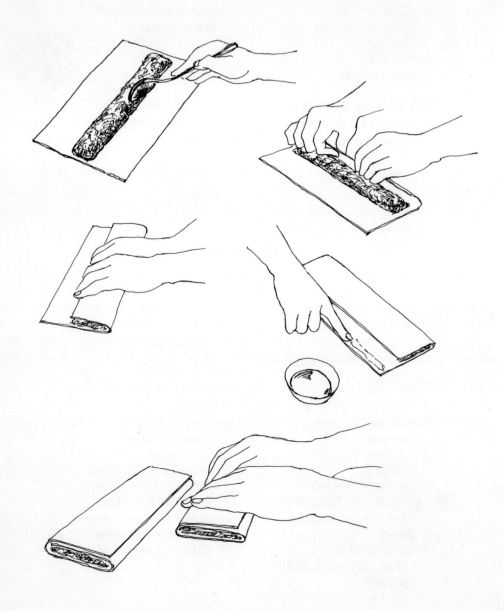

CHILLED TOFU WITH FOUR CHINESE SAUCES

(color plate 2)

These sauces really complement tofu's unique flavor. Try them all. Cut the tofu into a different shape for each sauce, chill, and serve topped with the sauces.

(serves 6–8)

1 ½ cakes "silk" tofu

dried shrimp sauce:
1 Tbsp vegetable oil
1 Tbsp sesame oil
¼ cup dried shrimp, soaked in boiling water for 10–15 minutes, drained, and finely chopped

1 clove garlic, finely chopped
½ lb mustard greens, par-boiled, squeezed, and finely chopped
pinch powdered ginger
1 Tbsp soy sauce
2 Tbsps saké

Heat vegetable and sesame oil in skillet and sauté shrimp and garlic for 1 minute. Add mustard greens, saké, and seasonings and continue to cook, stirring constantly, until liquid is absorbed.

hundred-year-old egg sauce:
1 Chinese "hundred-year-old" egg, shelled and finely chopped

1 tsp fresh ginger juice

Combine all ingredients.

Chinese pickle sauce:
½ cup Chinese pickles (*zha-cai*), washed and finely chopped
1 dried red pepper, seeded

and finely chopped (or ¼ tsp cayenne pepper)
1 Tbsp sesame oil
1 tsp saké
1 tsp soy sauce

Combine all ingredients.

meat sauce:
2–3 slices Chinese roast pork or Canadian bacon, finely chopped
½ cup seeded, finely chopped cucumber

1 small dried red pepper, seeded and finely chopped
3-ounce jar pimiento, drained and diced
2 Tbsps vegetable oil

Combine all ingredients.

TOFU FRUIT SQUARES
(color plate 3)

Tofu fruit squares are high in nutritive value and make a great snack.

(makes 24 squares)

syrup:
½ cup honey
1 Tbsp lemon juice
½ tsp fresh ginger juice or
¼ tsp powdered ginger

fruit (see below)
¼ cake tofu, drained by
Method I and cut into
1 × 1 × ¼-inch pieces

Combine syrup ingredients. Cut the fruit a little bigger than the tofu, top with tofu, and pour on a little syrup.

Any kind of fresh or canned fruit may be used, and syrup flavor may be adjusted to taste.

TOMATO TARTLETS
(color plate 3)

These tartlets are a delightful way to utilize summer's abundance of ripe tomatoes. The blending of tomato and tofu results in a refreshing creamy texture. It is important to use only fresh ripe tomatoes. These tartlets and the onion tartlets that follow complement each other well when served together.

(makes 12–15 tartlets)

pastry:
1½ cups all-purpose flour
¼ tsp salt
6 Tbsps butter
1 Tbsp shortening
1 small egg
1 Tbsp cold water

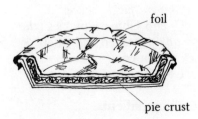

foil

pie crust

filling:
¼ cup grated Swiss cheese
2 medium-sized ripe
tomatoes, peeled, seeded,
and chopped
¼ cake tofu, drained by
Method II and cut into
½-inch cubes

⅛ tsp each dried basil and
pepper
½ tsp salt
2 Tbsps butter

pastry:

Sift flour and salt into a bowl. Cut in butter and shortening until mixture resembles coarse crumbs. Gradually stir in egg and water until mixture leaves sides of bowl. Gather into ball and flatten slightly. Chill 1 hour, wrapped in plastic wrap.

Roll out pastry ⅛-inch thick on lightly floured surface and cut into 2-inch circles. Press into tartlet tins and trim pastry flush with top. Prick bottoms in several places with fork. Chill 15 minutes.

Preheat oven to 400°F.

Line the inside of tartlet shells with foil and place tins on baking sheet. Bake until pastry is set, about 6–7 minutes. Remove foil and cool to room temperature. Reduce oven temperature to 375°F to bake filling.

filling:

Mix the cheese, tomato, tofu, and seasonings. Fill baked tartlet shells ¾ full and dot with butter. Bake until the cheese is melted and the tartlets are heated through, about 10–15 minutes.

Serve piping hot or at room temperature.

for 9-inch pie:

Pastry recipe need not be adjusted.

filling:	Method II and cut into
¾ cup grated Swiss cheese	½-inch cubes
4–5 large ripe tomatoes, peeled, seeded, and chopped	¼ tsp each dried basil and pepper
½ cake tofu, drained by	2 tsps salt
	3 Tbsps butter

Prepare filling as above and spoon into partially baked 9-inch pie shell. Bake at 375°F for 30 minutes. Serve hot oir at room temperature.

ONION TARTLETS

(color plate 3)

pastry:	Method II and mashed
tartlet shells (see p. 54)	1 Tbsp flour
	1 tsp salt
filling:	⅛ tsp each pepper and
3 Tbsps butter	dried thyme
1 medium onion, thinly sliced	1 medium egg
¼ cake tofu, drained by	¼ cup heavy cream
	¼ cup grated Swiss cheese

Preheat oven to 375°F.

Melt butter in skillet and sauté onion until soft but not brown. Add tofu, flour, and seasonings, and cook over low heat 2–3 minutes longer. Cool.

In a separate bowl, beat egg and then blend in cream. Add cheese and cooled onion mixture.

Fill baked tartlet shells ¾ full and bake at 375°F for 10–15 minutes or until golden brown.

for 9-inch pie:
Pastry recipe need not be adjusted.

filling:	2 tsps salt
4 Tbsps butter	¼ tsp each pepper and
1 Tbsp vegetable oil	dried thyme
3–4 medium onions, thinly	2 large eggs
sliced	⅔ cup heavy cream
½ cake tofu, drained by	½ cup grated Swiss cheese
Method II and mashed	

Prepare filling as above, pour into 9-inch partially baked pie shell and bake at 375°F for 30 minutes.

MEATBALLS
(color plate 3)

A combination of ground meat and tofu, these crisp meatballs make a good hors d'oeuvre.

For a variation, this recipe can also be used to make hamburger patties. Just add a little milk to the mixture, dredge with flour, and fry in butter. Serve sprinkled with a little soy sauce or a combination of soy sauce and butter.

(makes 20–25 meatballs)

2 Tbsps butter	⅛ tsp each pepper and
1 onion, finely chopped	nutmeg
½ lb ground beef	vegetable oil for deep-frying
½ cake tofu, drained by	finely chopped parsley (op-
Method I and lightly	tional garnish)
squeezed in cheesecloth	soy sauce and butter, heated
1 tsp salt	(optional)

Melt butter in skillet and sauté onion until soft. Transfer to mixing bowl and cool. Add beef, tofu, and seasonings and mix well. Form into 1-inch balls. Heat ½ inch oil in skillet to medium temperature (340°F). Deep-fry meatballs, keeping them moving in the oil, until golden brown. Drain on paper towels. Serve sprinkled with parsley. Accompany with soy sauce and butter if desired.

TOFU PUFFS
(color plate 3)

Delicate choux pastry is excellent for hors d'oeuvres. Here, the pastry puffs contain such surprises as cream cheese, crisp crumbs of bacon, and tofu. The puffs may also be filled with blue cheese morsels, minced walnuts and shallots, and tofu.

(makes about 30 puffs)

choux pastry:
1 cup water
¼ tsp salt
4 Tbsps butter
1 cup sifted flour
3 large eggs
1 cup grated Swiss cheese
⅛ tsp nutmeg

filling:
4 ounces cream cheese, at
   room temperature
2 slices bacon, fried until
   crisp, drained, and
   crumbled
¼ cake tofu, drained by
   Method II and cut into
   ½-inch cubes

Preheat oven to 450°F.

In a saucepan, bring the water, salt, and butter slowly to a boil. When butter is melted, remove pan from heat and immediately pour in all of the flour. Beat with a wooden spoon until smooth. Return to heat and continue beating over medium heat for 2 minutes to evaporate excess liquid.

Remove from heat and add one egg at a time, beating well after each addition. Add cheese and nutmeg; mix well. Fill pastry bag and squeeze 30 2-inch puffs onto a baking sheet, spacing them 2 inches apart.

Bake for 20 minutes or until puffs double in size. Turn off oven, open door slightly, and leave puffs inside for another 5 minutes to dry out.

Soften cream cheese and blend in bacon bits.

Cut puffs in half and place a small amount of tofu in the bottom. Top with cream cheese and bacon mixture. Replace top of puff.

Note: Puffs may be baked ahead; when cool, wrap well in plastic wrap and freeze. Thaw at room temperature and bake in a 350°F oven for 1 minute.

TOFU CHIPS

Tofu chips are unique! Although the process of draining the tofu can be difficult and time-consuming, the finished result is worth the effort. Tofu chips are an excellent substitute for crisp bacon crumbs in salads and sauces and can be used in a variety of ways that are guaranteed to appeal to the vegetarian and non-vegetarian alike. An exciting dressing can be made by recrisping and mincing tofu chips then adding them to French dressing seasoned with soy sauce.

(makes 2 cups)

½ cup vegetable oil
½ cake tofu, drained by
    Method III, cut into
    julienne strips, and wrap-
ped in clean kitchen towel
    to drain further
salt

Heat oil in frying pan and fry tofu over medium heat until crisp. Drain on paper towel and salt lightly.

Soups

VEGETARIAN TOFU SOUP
Kenchin Jiru I

Tofu sautéed in sesame oil is often added to soups. This is a classical Japanese recipe (*kenchin jiru*), which is actually closer to the Western idea of a stew than a soup. Other vegetables—for instance, potatoes and turnips—may be used in addition to those listed here. Though this is vegetarian, it would make the basis of a hearty dish if some kind of meat—pork, ham, or chicken, or oysters—is added. The following recipe is a version of this one using a light meat and easily available vegetables.

(serves 6)

2 Tbsps vegetable oil
1 Tbsp sesame oil
1 cake tofu, drained by Method II
3 dried *shiitake* mushrooms, reconstituted in warm water for 30 minutes, drained, stems removed, and thinly sliced
1 medium carrot, cut into julienne strips
7-inch piece burdock root (*gobō*), cut into julienne strips

1 cake *konnyaku*, rinsed with hot water and cut into $1/8$-inch slices
5 cups *dashi* (p. 24; use *kobu dashi* for strict vegetarians)
2 Tbsps soy sauce
2 tsps salt
4–6 Tbsps finely chopped chives or scallions

Heat vegetable and sesame oils in a heavy pot over medium heat. Sauté tofu for 5 minutes, crushing with a wooden spoon until crumbly. Add vegetables and *konnyaku* and stir well. Add *dashi* and bring to a boil. Skim top and add soy sauce and salt. Cover, reduce heat to low, and cook slowly for about 30 minutes. Add chives or scallions just before serving.

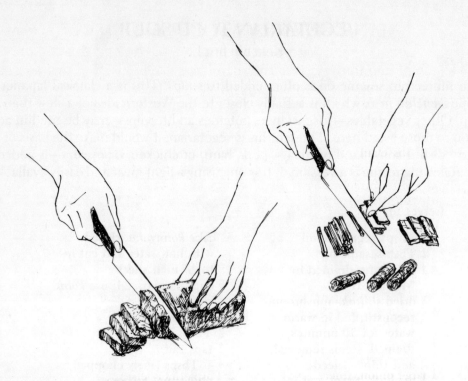

VEGETABLE AND TOFU SOUP WITH MEAT
Kenchin Jiru II

(serves 6)

2–3 Tbsps vegetable oil
1 Tbsp sesame oil (optional)
½ lb pork or chicken, cut
   diagonally into ½-inch
   slices
1–2 dashes powdered ginger
½ cake tofu, drained by
   Method II

2 medium potatoes, cut into
   ½-inch cubes
1 medium carrot, cut into
   ½-inch cubes
1 leek, thinly sliced
5 cups water
⅓ cup saké
3 Tbsps soy sauce
1 ½ tsps salt (to taste)

Heat oils over medium heat in a deep pot and sauté meat for 5–6 minutes or until lightly browned. Remove the meat, sprinkle it with powdered ginger, and set aside. Mash the tofu in the same pot with a wooden spoon while sautéing for 2–3 minutes. Add all vegetables and continue to sauté for 5–6 minutes or until the tofu becomes crumbly. Return the meat to the pot, add the water, and bring to a boil, skimming top. Add saké, soy sauce, and salt to taste. Cover and simmer for 30 minutes over medium-low heat.

MANHATTAN CLAM CHOWDER

The addition of tofu to this classic chowder makes it creamier and counteracts the acidity of the tomato while enhancing the flavor. The sound of the tofu being stirred in hot oil adds a bit of drama to the preparation of this recipe.

(serves 6)

2–3 lbs clams, scrubbed

steaming ingredients:
1/4 cup dry vermouth
1 sprig parsley
1 celery stalk, with leaves
1 tsp black peppercorns
2 cups water

2/3 cake tofu, drained by
    Method I and cut into
    1/2-inch cubes
1 Tbsp vegetable oil
2 Tbsps butter
1 large onion, finely
    chopped
1 clove garlic, finely
    chopped
3 Tbsps flour

3 medium tomatoes, peeled,
    seeded, and cut into
    1/2-inch pieces
1 stalk celery, diced
3 medium potatoes, diced
3 cups water
1 Tbsp salt
1/4 tsp pepper
1 bay leaf
1/2 tsp dried thyme (1 sprig
    fresh)
1/2 tsp dried dill weed (1
    sprig fresh)
2 cloves
2 Tbsps finely chopped
    parsley

Put clams in a pot with steaming ingredients. Cover tightly and steam over medium heat until the shells open—about 5, not more than 10, minutes. Remove the clams from their shells.

Strain the liquid and marinate clams while the rest of the chowder is being prepared.

Heat the oil and butter in a pot and sauté the onion and garlic over medium heat until soft but not browned—about 5–6 minutes. Add flour and stir for 1 minute. Add tofu, mashing and stirring vigorously with a wooden spoon. This is noisy. Stir constantly for 5–6 minutes. The color will deepen a little. Add tomatoes, celery, and potatoes and continue sautéing for another 2–3 minutes. Add 3 cups of water and bring to a boil over high heat. Skim and add the salt, pepper, and other seasonings. Cover and cook for 30 minutes over low heat. Adjust the flavor to taste, then add the clams along with liquid and continue cooking just long enough to heat them through, about 3–4 minutes.

Serve hot, garnished with the chopped parsley.

CHICKEN, OYSTER, AND TOFU GUMBO

Gumbo is a light stew, and tofu is a natural for it. Tofu is so good in gumbo, in fact, that you can eliminate the chicken and oysters if you like. Filé powder, usually used in true Louisiana gumbo, is hard to find, so it is omitted here.

(serves 6–8)

chicken and stock:
2 1/2–3 lb chicken, cleaned
1 onion, sliced
1 handful celery leaves
7 cups water
1 tsp salt
1/2 tsp cayenne pepper
1/4 cup dry white wine

1/2 cup vegetable oil
1/2 cup flour

1 large onion, chopped
4 cloves garlic, finely
   chopped
1/2 cup chopped green
   pepper
1 cup chopped celery
1/2 cake tofu, drained by
   Method II and cut into
   1/2-inch cubes
1 lb okra, thinly sliced
1 pint fresh oysters
1/3 cup finely chopped
   scallions or chives
1/2 cup finely chopped
   parsley
hot cooked rice

chicken and stock:
Place all ingredients in a pot and bring to a boil. Lower heat and simmer 20–30 minutes or until chicken is cooked. Remove chicken and let it cool. Skin and debone chicken and tear or cut it into bite-sized pieces. Strain stock. You should have 5 cups of chicken stock.

In a large saucepan or Dutch oven heat oil over medium-low heat and add flour. Cook, stirring constantly, until light brown. Take care not to burn. Add onion, garlic, peppers, and celery and sauté for 5–6 minutes. Gradually add 5 cups prepared chicken stock.

Bring to a boil and lower heat to medium. Simmer for 1/2 hour. Add chicken, tofu, and 1/2 of the okra and simmer 1/2 hour longer or until slightly thickened. Taste and adjust seasonings. Bring to a full boil and add oysters, scallions, parsley, and the remaining okra. Cover, remove from heat, and let stand 10–15 minutes. Serve over hot rice in soup bowls.

OYSTER STEW
(color plate 6)

Soy milk is substituted for conventional milk here. This was done to satisfy my curiosity when trying out recipes for this book, and the results are worth sharing. Soy milk, though quite different in flavor from cow's milk, complements the oysters deliciously and also provides vegetable protein.

(serves 6)

5 cups soy milk
1 lb oysters, rinsed well and
    drained
2 tsps salt

1/2 tsp pepper
2 Tbsps butter
nutmeg

Heat the soy milk in a pot and add the oysters. Bring just to boiling point then simmer for 3 minutes over low heat while skimming top. Season with salt and pepper and add butter. Pour into preheated bowls and sprinkle with nutmeg.

CONSOMMÉ WITH GREEN DUMPLINGS

Tofu makes an excellent base for dumplings—it gives both nutrition and flavor. Here spinach is used, but anything goes (see variation below). Try tofu dumplings in your next chicken stew or, boiled and sautéed, next to roast meat.

(serves 6)

dumpling batter:
1/2 cake tofu, drained by
    Method III
3/4 lb spinach, parboiled and
    squeezed of moisture
2 medium eggs
2 cups bread crumbs
1 tsp salt
1/2 tsp white pepper
1/2 tsp nutmeg

1 tsp salt

consommé:
4 cups chicken stock
salt and pepper to taste

3-4 Tbsps grated Parmesan
    cheese
2 Tbsps finely chopped
    parsley

Mix dumpling batter ingredients (or process in a food processor or blender for 1-2 minutes) to get a thick batter. Bring about 3 inches of water and 1 tsp salt to a boil in a large pot. Lower heat to just below boiling and drop in dumpling batter 1 Tbsp at a time. After 2-3 minutes, the dumplings will start to float. Drain. Repeat until all batter has been used. Heat the chicken stock to boiling. Add salt and pepper to taste. Add dumplings, lower the heat, and simmer for 3-4 minutes until the dumplings are heated through.

Serve in individual soup bowls; sprinkle with Parmesan cheese and chopped parsley.

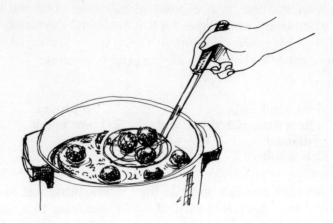

Variation: ¼ lb calf's liver, sautéed then pureed, mixed with ¼ of the dumpling mixture and used as a filling in the center of the dumplings is delicious.

SUMMER VEGETABLE STEW

Somehow certain vegetables have come to be classed exclusively as "salad greens," and it seems odd to cook them. In Oriental cooking, the line between raw and cooked vegetables is very fine—green vegetables are young, tender, and delicate, and they are never cooked beyond crispness. Also, which greens are eaten raw and which are cooked is not an issue. That is why I have introduced this recipe. The lettuce used in this stew gives it the refreshing taste of early summer, while the combination of tofu and vegetables is equally refreshing.

(serves 6)

¼ cup olive oil
1 cup sliced onion
5–6 cups chicken stock
1 cup diced carrot
2 cups diced potato
1 head cauliflower, flowerets separated and sliced
1 celery stalk, diced
½ cup green peas
½ cup chopped green beans

1 tsp dried basil
2 tsps salt
pepper to taste
5–6 lettuce leaves, roughly shredded
2–3 Tbsps olive oil
1 cake "cotton" tofu, drained by Method III and cut into 12 2×1×½-inch pieces
1 Tbsp finely chopped parsley

In a large saucepan, heat olive oil and sauté onion until soft but not browned. Add chicken stock and bring to a boil. Add all vegetables except lettuce and season with basil, salt, and pepper. Cover and cook 30 minutes over medium-low heat, skimming off foam. Just before serving, add lettuce and bring to a boil.

When the soup is nearly ready, heat olive oil in skillet and fry tofu slices on both sides until light brown. Place two slices in each soup plate, add soup, and garnish with chopped parsley.

HOT AND SOUR SOUP
(color plate 4)

This is a soup from the Sichuan Province of China. It is important to cut the tofu into long, thin slices, and to take care that it keeps its shape and does not come apart during preparation. If it does, the soup will take on an unpleasant cloudy quality. The beaten egg should be stirred in at the very end.

The idea of a combination of hot and sour may be a little off-putting at first, but do be adventurous and try it. I guarantee it will soon become a firm favorite.

(serves 6–8)

3–4 Tbsps vegetable oil
1/4 cup finely chopped
   scallions or chives
1 tsp finely chopped fresh
   ginger root
1 clove garlic, finely
   chopped
1/2 lb pork loin, cut into
   julienne strips
4 dried *shiitake* mushrooms,
   reconstituted in warm
   water for 30 minutes,
   drained, stems removed,
   and thinly sliced
1/2 cup shredded bamboo
   shoot

2 dried red peppers, seeded
   and chopped
5 cups chicken or beef stock
1/2 cup saké
2 Tbsps soy sauce
1 tsp salt
1 tsp pepper
1/2 cup rice vinegar
2 Tbsps cornstarch dissolved
   in 1/2 cup cold stock
1 cake tofu, drained by
   Method II and cut into
   julienne strips
1 egg, beaten
1 Tbsp red pepper oil

Heat vegetable oil over medium heat in a wok and sauté scallions, ginger root, garlic, and pork until pork is browned. Add *shiitake* mushrooms, bamboo shoot, red pepper, stock, and saké. Bring to a boil and cook for 6–7 minutes, skimming top. Season with soy sauce, salt, and pepper, then cook over medium heat for another 5–6 minutes. Add vinegar, cornstarch, and tofu. Pour in beaten egg and mix well as it cooks. The chili oil is added just before removing from heat.

The soup is served hot. Those who like it even hotter and/or sourer can add red pepper oil and vinegar to taste.

WAKAME SEAWEED AND GINGER SOUP

(color plate 4)

This clear soup base with *wakame* seaweed and needle shreds of ginger added just before serving is a subtle combination of delicate and vigorous flavors. It will please almost anyone and may well become a part of your repertoire for parties and family fare.

(serves 6)

5 cups *dashi* (see p. 24)
½ cup saké
2 tsps salt
1 Tbsp lard
½ cup *wakame* seaweed,
   reconstituted in hot water,
   hard parts trimmed away,
   and cut into bite-sized
   pieces
1 cake tofu, cut into
   $1 \times 1 \times 1/2$-inch pieces
2 Tbsps finely shred-cut
   fresh ginger root

Place *dashi*, saké, salt, lard, and *wakame* seaweed in pot and bring to a boil. Skim top and add tofu. Cook for 5–6 minutes.

Pour soup into individual bowls and sprinkle with fine shreds of fresh ginger root.

SCALLOP SOUP

(color plate 4)

Scallops and wood ears blend well in this tasty soup. Cooking enhances the flavor of the cucumber, which adds a fresh green accent, while a contrast in color and flavor is provided by the yellow of the chrysanthemum petals.

(serves 6)

- 1 Tbsp vegetable oil
- 2 Tbsps sliced scallions or chives
- 1 tsp finely chopped fresh ginger root
- 5–6 dried scallops, washed and soaked in ½ cup hot water (reserve the water)
- 1 small bamboo shoot, thinly sliced
- ½ cup wood ears, reconstituted in warm water and cut into bite-sized pieces
- 5 cups Chinese soup stock (see p. 24)
- ¼ cup saké
- 1 tsp soy sauce
- 2 tsps salt
- pepper to taste
- 1 small cucumber, thinly sliced
- ½ cake tofu, cut into ½×1×¼-inch pieces
- dried yellow chrysanthemum petals (optional), reconstituted in water

Heat oil over medium heat in a wok and sauté scallions, ginger root, and scallops for 2 minutes. Add bamboo shoot, wood ears, soup stock, saké, and water in which scallops were soaked. Cook over medium heat for 10 minutes. Season with soy sauce, salt, and pepper. Add cucumber and tofu and cook another 2 minutes.

If dried yellow chrysanthemum petals or small yellow chrysanthemum flowers are available, these can be added just before removing from heat. They provide an attractive color contrast to the tofu.

STEAMED SAVORY CUSTARD
Chawan mushi   (color plate 8)

Traditional egg custards in Japan are always dishes that are full of surprises, rich in the fruits of the seas and rivers, and the fields and mountains. The delights change with the seasons but can include shrimp, pieces of fish, scallops, pieces of chicken, nuts, mushrooms, and leafy green vegetables. The egg custard I have chosen to introduce here has tofu as its main filling and is extremely palatable and light. It can be eaten either hot or cold, and you can experiment by ringing the seasonal changes, for example, using chestnuts in the fall, or paper-thin slices of cucumber in the summer.

(serves 4)

- *egg custard:*
- 3 medium eggs
- 2½ cups *dashi* (see p. 24)
- ⅔ tsp salt
- 2 Tbsps saké
- 1 tsp soy sauce
- ½ cake tofu, cut into quarters
- 4 shrimp, shelled and blanched in lightly salted water
- 4 ginkgo nuts

Beat eggs lightly without forming bubbles. Add *dashi*, salt, saké, and soy sauce. Strain through a fine sieve.

Place a piece of tofu and custard mixture in individual cups and top each with a shrimp and a ginkgo nut.

Cover tightly with aluminum foil. Steam over medium heat for 20 minutes or until knife inserted in the center comes out clean.

(If baking instead of steaming, preheat oven to 400°F. Place custard cups in a baking dish and pour in enough tepid water to come halfway up the sides of the cups. Cook for 20 minutes.)

MISO SOUP WITH TOFU
(color plate 5)

Miso soup (*miso shiru*) is one of the pillars of Japanese cooking. Basically *miso shiru* is made by diluting *miso*, a savory, fermented soybean paste, in stock. There are so many types of *miso* that, with additions of other ingredients, you can make an almost limitless number of soups.

One of the basic *miso* soups includes small squares of tofu and one or more vegetables. Despite radical changes in life-style and diet in Japan, *miso* soup remains firmly fixed in Japanese daily fare because its versatility allows it to be served at any meal.

You can adjust the taste of *miso* soup by altering the amount of *miso* you use or by combining two different varieties of *miso* to create a soup that is unique to your table.

(serves 6)

5 cups *dashi* (see p. 24)	½ cake tofu, cut into
6 Tbsps red *miso*	½-inch cubes
	1 okra pod, thinly sliced

Heat the *dashi* in a pot. Melt the *miso* in ¼ cup warm *dashi*, then strain this *miso* mixture into the pot of *dashi*. Stir until blended. Gently add the tofu. Warm over medium heat, but do not bring to a boil, because it will lose flavor.

Place a few slices of okra in each lacquered soup bowl and add the hot soup. Serve immediately.

Main Dishes

BEEF ROLLS WITH TOFU STUFFING
(color plate 7)

The feature of this recipe is the stuffing. The mixture of scrambled tofu and egg is light in contrast to the beef, yet it is rich and complements the flavor of the meat.

(serves 6)

½ cake tofu, drained by
   Method II and mashed
3 large eggs
⅓ cup heavy cream
1 Tbsp flour
1 tsp salt
pepper to taste
⅛ tsp nutmeg
3 Tbsps butter
6 thin 3×4-inch beef slices
½ tsp each salt and pepper
⅓–½ cup flour
3 Tbsps butter
1 Tbsp vegetable oil

sauce:
2 Tbsps butter

1 medium onion, thinly
   sliced
1 stalk celery, thinly sliced
1 clove garlic, thinly sliced
1 Tbsp flour
½ cup dry vermouth
1½ cups chicken stock
2 Tbsps tomato paste
1 bay leaf
⅛ tsp dried thyme
1 tsp salt
¼ tsp pepper

1 cup sour cream
1–2 Tbsps finely chopped
   parsley

Beat tofu, eggs, cream, flour, salt, pepper, and nutmeg until smooth. Heat butter in pan and scramble egg-tofu mixture. Cool.

Season beef slices with salt and pepper. Divide the scrambled egg mixture into six parts and stuff beef slices, rolling and tying each firmly with string. Dredge with flour. Heat butter and oil in skillet and brown beef on all sides over medium heat. Remove from pan and set aside.

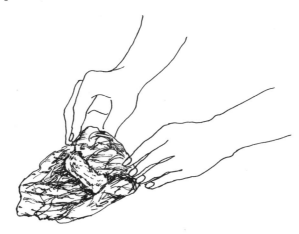

Add butter to pan juices and sauté onion, celery, and garlic until golden brown. Add flour and continue sautéing for 2 minutes. Add remaining ingredients except sour cream and parsley. Cover and simmer over low heat for 15 minutes, then remove from heat and press through sieve or food mill. Return sauce to pan and taste for seasoning. Add beef and cook, covered, over low heat 10–15 minutes longer or until sauce is reduced to 1½ cups.

Remove string from beef and serve with sauce, topping each portion with approximately 2 Tbsps sour cream and finely chopped parsley to taste.

TOFU-AND-MEAT LOAF EN CROÛTE

Ground beef, tofu, and cream cheese here create an interesting and rich—and unusual—loaf. Ordinary meat loaf is family fare, but this dish is for festive occasions.

(serves 6)

pastry:
2 cups sifted flour
$\frac{1}{2}$ tsp salt
4 Tbsps butter
1 large egg
$\frac{1}{3}$ cup sour cream

filling:
4 Tbsps butter
2 medium onions, finely chopped
$\frac{1}{2}$ lb mushrooms, sliced
1 lb ground beef
$\frac{1}{3}$ cup flour
2 tsps salt
pepper to taste
$\frac{1}{2}$ tsp nutmeg

1 cake tofu, drained by Method II
8 ounces cream cheese, cut into 1-inch cubes
$\frac{1}{4}$ cup finely chopped parsley

glaze:
1 egg yolk
2 Tbsps water

1 cup sour cream

pastry:
Sift flour and salt together, then rub in butter with fingertips until mixture resembles coarse crumbs. Blend in the egg and sour cream. Form into a ball, wrap in plastic wrap, and chill for 1 hour.

filling:
Melt butter in a saucepan and sauté onions until soft. Add mushrooms and beef and cook until meat is no longer pink. Sprinkle on the flour and seasonings and cook until thickened. Remove from heat, mix in tofu, cream cheese, and parsley, and cool.

Preheat oven to 375°F.
    Roll pastry into a 16×14-inch rectangle. Divide vertically in two, with one piece slightly larger than the other. Place the smaller piece on a baking sheet and mound the meat filling in the center. Moisten edges of the crust with water. Cover with the larger piece, press edges together firmly, and round the corners to form a snug shape around filling. Turn up the edges, fold in, and crimp with fork.
    Mix the egg yolk and water and brush top of loaf. Pierce the crust in a few places, then bake for 50 minutes.
    Slide very carefully onto heated platter. Serve hot with sour cream in a separate bowl.

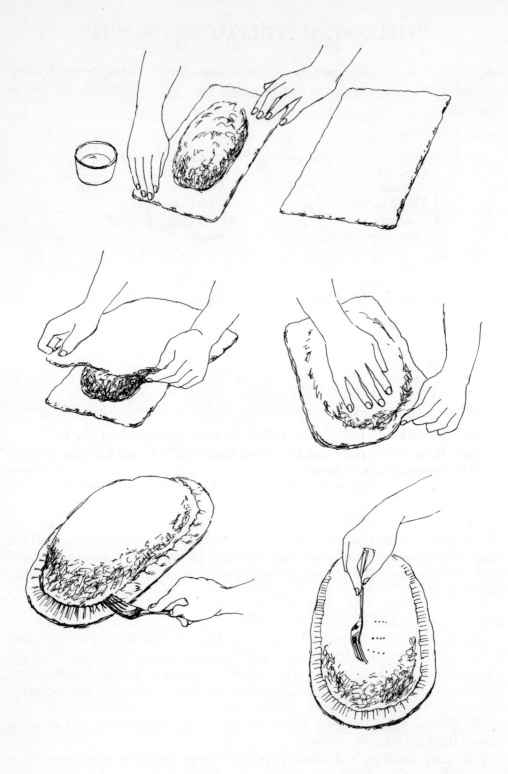

SPINACH QUICHE

(color plate 17)

Tofu may be pureed and used in the basic custard mix, may be included cut in cubes or slices, or may be sautéed until crisp, as is done here, and included in any quiche. It is a marvelous addition.

(serves 6)

10-inch pastry shell (see p. 148)

filling:
2–4 Tbsps vegetable oil
½ cake tofu, drained by Method II, cut in half lengthwise and then crosswise into ½-inch slices
4 Tbsps butter
1 Tbsp finely chopped scallions or chives
1 lb fresh or 10-ounce box

frozen spinach, parboiled in lightly salted water, squeezed, and chopped (approximately 1 cup)
1 tsp salt
⅛ tsp pepper
2 large eggs
⅔ cup heavy cream
½ tsp salt
⅛ tsp each pepper and nutmeg
½ cup grated Swiss cheese
1 Tbsp butter

Preheat oven to 400°F.

Cover pie shell with foil, place a slightly smaller pie plate on top, and bake for 8 minutes. Remove top plate and foil, lower heat to 375°F, and bake for an additional 8–10 minutes, until done.

While the crust is baking, heat 2–4 Tbsps oil in a skillet and lightly brown the tofu slices on both sides.

Melt 4 Tbsps butter and sauté scallions for 1 minute. Add spinach, salt, and pepper and sauté, stirring, for 5–6 minutes over low heat. Set aside to cool.

Beat eggs and mix in cream, salt, pepper, nutmeg, all but 1 Tbsp cheese, and spinach. Place the tofu slices in the pastry shell and cover with the spinach mixture. Sprinkle 1 Tbsp cheese on top and dot with butter. Bake for 30 minutes. Serve hot or at room temperature.

custard
tofu

SHRIMP QUENELLES AU GRATIN

(color plate 7)

Well, why not use tofu in quenelles? The result speaks for itself.

(serves 6)

½ recipe choux paste (see p. 57)	*sauce:*
	4 Tbsps butter
½ cake tofu, drained by Method II and mashed	3 Tbsps flour
	1 cup milk
½ lb shrimp, shelled and deveined	½ tsp salt
	pepper
¼ tsp nutmeg	
1 tsp salt	2–3 Tbsps grated cheese
	1 Tbsp butter

Place choux paste, tofu, shrimp, nutmeg, and salt in blender or food processor and process until smooth—approximately 2–3 minutes. Form into 1-inch balls and drop into a pan of rapidly boiling water. As the balls rise to the surface, remove with a slotted spoon. Save 1 cup of poaching liquid for the gratin sauce.

Preheat oven to 350°F.

Melt butter over medium-low heat. Add flour and cook for 1 minute without browning. With a wire whisk, stir in milk, 1 cup of poaching liquid, salt, and pepper until sauce is smooth. Cook on low heat for about 10 minutes, stirring occasionally.

Butter a 10-inch gratin dish. Place shrimp quenelles on bottom, cover with sauce, and sprinkle with grated cheese. Dot with butter and bake 25–30 minutes or until bubbly hot.

TOFU CURRY GRATIN

Here tofu is fried in oil until the surface forms a golden brown coat over the creamy interior. It is important that the tofu keep its shape and the center remain moist, so be careful not to overcook it. If you omit the white sauce, this is a delicious pilaff-like dish.

(8-inch pie)

2 Tbsps vegetable oil
1 cake tofu, drained by
   Method II and cut into
   1/2-inch cubes
4 Tbsps butter
1/2 cup finely chopped
   celery
1 cup finely chopped onion
2 cups cooked rice
2 tsps curry powder
salt and pepper to taste

1 Tbsp butter
1 1/2–2 cups white sauce
   (below)
2 Tbsps grated Swiss cheese

white sauce:
3 Tbsps butter
2 Tbsps flour
2 cups milk
2–3 Tbsps dry vermouth
1/2 tsp salt
dash white pepper

Preheat oven to 350°F.

Heat vegetable oil over medium heat in a frying pan. Lightly brown tofu cubes and set aside.

Add 2 Tbsps of butter to the pan and sauté celery and onion for 2–3 minutes. Add 1 Tbsp of butter and rice and sauté for 4–5 minutes. Add curry powder, salt, and pepper. Remove from heat and add sautéed tofu. Toss lightly.

white sauce:

Melt butter over low heat. Blend in the flour and cook slowly, stirring, for 2 minutes without browning. Add 1/2 cup milk and stir with a wire whisk until well blended. Add remaining milk, vermouth, and seasonings and cook for 5 minutes.

Grease 8-inch pie plate with 1 Tbsp butter. Fill with rice and tofu mixture, cover with white sauce, and top with cheese. Bake 30 minutes. Serve hot.

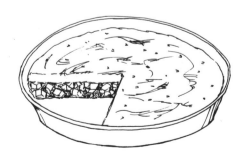

TOFU CASSEROLE

Here the standard American tuna casserole has been enhanced by the addition of tofu and a slightly richer sauce because I wanted to show just how versatile tofu can be. Simmered and sliced chicken breast, cooked and flaked white-meat fish, clams, or smoked salmon may be added to this quickly assembled and cooked casserole dish.

(serves 6–8)

1/4 cup cornmeal
2 cakes tofu, drained by
   Method II, cut into
   quarters then into 1/2-inch
   slices
3 Tbsps vegetable oil
2 Tbsps butter

sauce:
3 Tbsps butter
1 cup thinly sliced onion
1 clove garlic, thinly sliced
2 Tbsps flour

2 1/2 cups milk
1 tsp salt
pinch pepper
1/4 tsp nutmeg
1/4 cup dry vermouth
1 cup sliced mushrooms

3 medium potatoes, cut into
   1/2-inch slices
breadcrumbs (or wheat germ
   or poppy seeds)
2 Tbsps butter

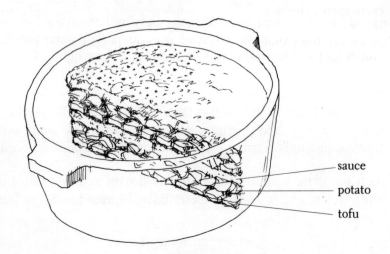

sauce

potato

tofu

Sprinkle cornmeal over tofu slices. Heat oil and butter in skillet over medium heat and fry tofu gently on both sides until lightly browned. Drain on paper towels.

Preheat oven to 350°F.

In separate pan make the sauce. Melt the butter and sauté onion and garlic until soft. Sprinkle in the flour and cook 1 minute. Add milk slowly, stirring constantly, then season with salt, pepper, and nutmeg. Add dry vermouth and mushrooms. Cook over medium heat 5–6 minutes or until thickened, stirring constantly.

Butter a 2-quart casserole, lay half the tofu slices on the bottom, followed by half the potato slices, then cover with half the white sauce. Repeat, sprinkle bread crumbs (or wheat germ or poppy seeds) over top, and dot with butter. Bake, covered, for 30 minutes. Uncover and bake 20 minutes longer or until nicely browned. Serve hot.

TOFU-TUNA-POTATO PATTIES

Here is a great use for leftover mashed potatoes. However you do this, it is home cooking. The tuna can go, if you like, and such things as crushed walnuts and toasted sesame seeds, parboiled and chopped spinach, mushrooms, boiled egg, diced cheese, ham, soft-cooked and chopped squid, and even truffles can be used.

(serves 6)

4 Tbsps butter
1 cup finely chopped onion
1 clove garlic, finely
   chopped
7-ounce can tuna, drained
   and flaked
2 medium potatoes, boiled
   and mashed
1/2 cake tofu, drained by
   Method II and mashed

1 large egg
1 Tbsp finely chopped
   parsley
1 1/2 tsps salt
1/8 tsp each pepper and
   nutmeg
1/2 cup flour
2 Tbsps vegetable oil

Melt 1 Tbsp butter in a frying pan and sauté onion and garlic until soft. Cool.

In a large mixing bowl mix tuna, potatoes, tofu, egg, cooled onion and garlic, parsley, and seasonings by hand. Add flour and blend well. Form into 2-inch patties.

Heat remaining 3 Tbsps butter and oil in frying pan and fry patties until golden brown on both sides. Serve hot or at room temperature.

Leftover patties make a hearty sandwich filling.

VEAL STEW

(color plate 7)

In Japanese cuisine, *oden* is perhaps the dish that most nearly simulates the Western stew. *Oden* is part of the winter household menu in Japan. Ingredients include vegetables in season, fish quenelles, hard-boiled eggs, and fish paste sausages stuffed with fragrant vegetables and deep-fried. No *oden* dish would be thought complete without grilled tofu and a variety of tofu products. These ingredients are stewed in a delicately flavored stock over low heat for a long time.

I have tried creating a stew that is low in calories for those who are concerned about their weight by using lean veal.

There are two ways of keeping the tofu from becoming tough. One is simply to warm it enough to heat through; the other is to simmer it a long time. Here, the tofu is simmered. Tofu is not a necessary ingredient here, but it is delicious and contributes to the flavor of the dish as well as its low-calorie virtue.

(serves 6)

3 Tbsps butter
1 lb veal, cut into 1-inch cubes and seasoned with salt and pepper
2 carrots, cut into 1-inch strips
1–1 1/2 lbs turnips, cut in half
1 cake tofu, drained by Method II and cut into 1-inch cubes

10 pearl onions (or 2 medium onions, quartered)
1 1/2 tsps salt
pepper to taste
1 bay leaf
4 cups beef stock
1/2 lb broccoli flowerets

Melt butter in large pot and brown veal. Add all remaining ingredients except broccoli and simmer 40 minutes, covered, skimming off fat. Add broccoli and cook 10 minutes longer, uncovered. Serve hot.

TOFU STEAK

(color plate 16)

Tofu steaks, sautéed in butter and served with a mushroom sauce, are quick and easy to prepare. Who knows, it may serve as an alternative to beef steak.

(serves 4)

2 cakes tofu, drained by Method I and cut in half lengthwise	2–3 shallots, finely chopped
	1 lb mushrooms, sliced
½ tsp salt	½ tsp salt
⅛ tsp pepper	⅛ tsp pepper
5 Tbsps vegetable oil	2 Tbsps butter, at room temperature
sauce:	2 Tbsps finely chopped parsley
3–4 Tbsps butter	

Season tofu lightly with salt and pepper. Heat 2 Tbsps of oil in skillet and sauté 2 tofu steaks at a time until golden brown on first side, shaking the pan frequently to prevent sticking. Turn carefully, using 2 spatulas, and sauté another 3 minutes. Repeat with remaining steaks. Transfer to a very hot serving platter and keep warm.

Melt butter and sauté shallots 1–2 minutes. Add mushrooms and sauté 3 minutes longer. Season with salt and pepper. Remove from heat and add softened butter. Top each tofu steak with sauce and garnish with chopped parsley. Serve hot.

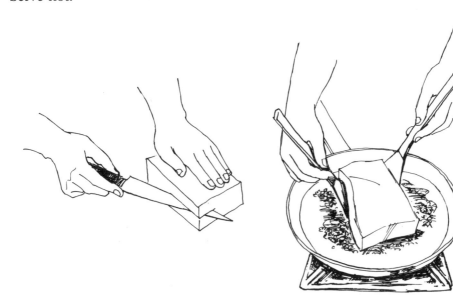

TOFU TERIYAKI

(serves 6)

$1/3$ cup soy sauce	$1 1/2$ cakes tofu, drained by
$1/4$ cup saké	Method I and cut into six
$1/4$ tsp pepper	pieces
	4 Tbsps butter

Mix soy sauce, saké, and pepper in a shallow container and marinate tofu for about 30 minutes, turning it once or twice. Reserve the marinade for later use.

Melt 2 Tbsps of butter in a skillet and sauté 3 pieces tofu over medium heat for 3 minutes on each side. Liquid will seep from the tofu as it heats, and it will seem to be simmering in the butter and liquid. Shake the skillet gently to prevent sticking. When lightly glazed, remove to a warm plate and repeat with the remaining butter and tofu.

Bring the reserved marinade to a boil over high heat and pour over the sautéed tofu before serving. Serve hot.

TOFU-POTATO DUMPLINGS

(serves 6)

1 cake tofu, drained by	1 large egg
Method II	$1/2$ cup flour
4 medium potatoes,	$1 1/2$ tsps salt
quartered, boiled, and	$1/2$ tsp pepper
drained	$1/4$ tsp nutmeg

Process all ingredients in a blender or food processor to a thick batter. Bring 2–3 inches of water to just below boiling in a large pot. Oil your hands and, taking $1/12$ of the batter (divide in fourths, then each fourth into thirds) at a time, shape into balls and drop into the water. The dumplings are done when they float. Remove and drain well. Serve with beef stew, gravy, or buttered bread crumbs.*

*Sauté 3 Tbsps bread crumbs and chopped parsley in 3 Tbsps butter until light brown. Season with salt and pepper.

STUFFED GREEN PEPPERS

Here is another example of how tofu enlivens and enriches a common, everyday dish.

(serves 6)

tofu-egg mixture:
1/2 cup tofu, drained by Method III
1 large egg
1 cup cooked rice
1 1/2 tsps salt
1/2 tsp pepper

vegetable mixture:
2 Tbsps olive oil
1 medium onion, finely chopped
1 medium stalk celery, finely chopped

1 clove garlic, finely chopped
1/2 lb mushrooms, finely chopped
1/2 tsp salt
1/4 tsp pepper

12 medium green peppers, cut in half lengthwise
flour
1 tsp each finely chopped fresh (or 1/2 tsp dried) parsley and basil
2 Tbsps olive oil

Blend all tofu-egg mixture ingredients in a food processor or blender until just mixed. The rice grains should remain whole (at least most of them). Heat 2 Tbsps olive oil in a pan and sauté the onion, celery, garlic, and mushrooms over medium-low heat until tender. Season with salt and pepper and set aside to cool. Lightly dust green pepper halves with flour. Combine the tofu-egg and vegetable mixtures, add the chopped parsley and basil, and mix well. Stuff the peppers.

Heat 2 Tbsps of olive oil in a frying pan. Add a single layer of peppers, stuffing side up. Cover and cook over medium heat for 4–5 minutes. Turn the peppers over and fry, uncovered, for an additional 3–4 minutes or until stuffing is browned. Repeat until all are done. Serve.

RATATOUILLE

Ratatouille is a versatile dish and is good served hot or cold. In this elegant version, I have added tofu sautéed in olive oil to the traditional recipe, which gives it an interesting texture and depth of flavor. I have found that it will also make an excellent hors d'oeuvre if you prepare it with the tofu and eggplant, but without the tomato sauce. It is delicious chilled and served on crisply toasted French bread.

(serves 6)

1 eggplant (about 1 lb), cut
   in half lengthwise and
   then into ¼-inch slices
1 tsp salt
4 Tbsps olive oil
1 cake tofu, drained by
   Method III and sliced
   same as eggplant

tomato sauce:
2–3 Tbsps olive oil
1 medium onion, finely
   chopped
2 cloves garlic, finely
   chopped

3 green peppers, chopped
4 medium-sized ripe toma-
   toes, peeled, seeded, and
   chopped
1 tsp salt
pepper to taste
¼ tsp dried basil

1 clove garlic, finely
   chopped
1 Tbsp finely chopped
   parsley
¼ tsp dried oregano

Sprinkle eggplant with 1 tsp salt and let stand for about 30 minutes. Rinse and pat dry.

Heat 2 Tbsps olive oil in a saucepan. Sauté eggplant on both sides until light brown, adding oil as needed. Remove eggplant from pan and drain on paper towels.

Sauté tofu slices in the same way as eggplant.

Heat 2–3 Tbsps olive oil and sauté onion and garlic until soft. Add green pepper, tomatoes, salt, pepper, and basil. Cover and cook over low heat for 20–30 minutes.

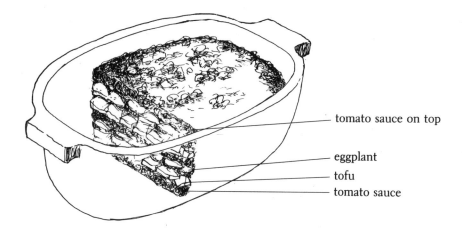

tomato sauce on top

eggplant
tofu
tomato sauce

Combine garlic, parsley, and oregano.

Butter a 2-quart casserole and pour in ⅓ of tomato sauce. Add a layer of tofu slices, sprinkle lightly with pepper, and add layer of eggplant. Sprinkle with ½ of garlic, parsley, and oregano mixture. Repeat layers, ending with remaining ⅓ of tomato sauce.

Preheat oven to 350°F.

Bake 30 minutes, uncovered. Serve hot or at room temperature.

MUSHROOM-STUFFED EGGPLANT

Eggplant and oil make beautiful harmony together. The addition of tofu gives deep richness to this easily prepared dish. Except for the butter and decorative sprinkling of cheese at the end, which are easily omitted, this is vegetarian.

(serves 6)

2 small eggplants (or 6 small Japanese eggplants)
1 Tbsp salt
3–4 Tbsps olive oil
¼ cup hot water
2 Tbsps each olive oil and butter
1 medium onion, finely chopped
⅓ lb mushrooms, finely chopped
2 Tbsps pine nuts

½ cake "cotton" tofu, drained by Method II
2 Tbsps finely chopped parsley
¼ tsp dried basil
salt and pepper to taste
2 Tbsps grated Swiss cheese (optional)
2–3 Tbsps bread crumbs
2 Tbsps butter (optional)
¼ cup water
paprika

Heat oven to 350°F.

Cut eggplants in half lengthwise. Sprinkle with salt and set aside 30 minutes. Rinse off salt and squeeze out water.

Pour olive oil in a baking dish or Dutch oven and heat in oven. Place eggplant cut side down in hot oil and add ¼ cup hot water. Cover with foil and bake for 20 minutes. Remove from oven and cool.

Scoop out flesh from cooked eggplant, leaving as thin a shell as possible. Chop eggplant flesh finely and place in bowl.

Heat 2 Tbsps each olive oil and butter over medium heat in a skillet. Add onion and mushroom and sauté until onion is soft but not brown. Add eggplant and pine nuts and sauté briefly. Add tofu, parsley, and basil and mix. Season to taste with salt and pepper.

Place stuffing in each eggplant shell. Sprinkle with grated cheese and bread crumbs. Dot with butter if you desire.

Place eggplant halves in a baking dish, stuffed side up, pour ¼ cup water into bottom of dish, and bake at 350°F for 20 minutes.

Serve hot, sprinkled with paprika.

TOFU AND TOMATO SPAGHETTI SAUCE

(serves 6)

1/3 cup olive oil	1/2 lb mushrooms, sliced
1 medium carrot, finely chopped	1/2 cup chopped black olives
1 medium onion, finely chopped	3 or 4 medium-sized ripe tomatoes, peeled, seeded, and chopped
1 medium stalk celery, finely chopped	1/3 cup tomato paste
2 cloves garlic, finely chopped	1 Tbsp salt
	1/2 tsp pepper
1 cake tofu, drained by Method I	1/2 tsp dried basil
	1/2 tsp dried oregano

Heat the oil in a heavy pot and sauté carrot, onion, celery, and garlic for 4–5 minutes. When the onions are translucent, stir in the tofu, crushing it with a spatula. Continue stir-frying for an additional 4–5 minutes, or until all ingredients are well blended and the tofu is crumbly and moist looking. Add the remaining ingredients. Cover partially and simmer for 30–40 minutes, stirring occasionally, or until desired thickness is obtained.

LASAGNE BOLOGNESE

Like spaghetti sauce, anything goes with lasagne, as long as it tastes good. Tofu tastes good here, where it is used instead of ricotta cheese. If you like, add some julienne strips of thin deep-fried tofu (*abura-age*).

(serves 6)

meat sauce:
- 4 Tbsps olive oil
- 4 Tbsps butter
- 1 clove garlic, finely chopped
- 1 medium onion, chopped
- 1 stalk celery, chopped
- 1/3 cup chopped black olives
- 2/3 lb chicken livers, chopped
- 3/4 lb ground pork
- 3/4 lb ground beef
- 1 1/2 lbs tomatoes, peeled, seeded, and chopped
- 1/4 cup tomato sauce
- 2 tsps salt
- 1/4 tsp each dried oregano, basil, and pepper
- 1/4 lb pepperoni, sliced
- Tabasco sauce to taste

mushrooms:
- 1 Tbsp olive oil
- 1/2 lb mushrooms, sliced
- 2 cloves garlic, sliced
- 1/2 tsp salt
- 1/4 tsp pepper
- 3 Tbsps finely chopped parsley

spinach:
4–6 Tbsps butter
1 medium onion, chopped
1 clove garlic, finely
  chopped
1 lb spinach, parboiled,
  squeezed, and chopped
½ tsp salt
¼ tsp pepper
2–3 Tbsps finely chopped
  parsley
½ cup heavy cream

¾ lb lasagne noodles, cooked according to package
  directions, drained, and
  rinsed in cold water
1 cake tofu, drained by
  Method II and mashed

meat sauce
pasta
tofu
meat sauce
pasta
spinach
pasta
mushrooms
pasta
tofu
meat sauce
pasta
meat sauce

meat sauce:
Heat olive oil and butter and sauté garlic, onion, and celery until soft. Add black olives, chicken livers, pork, and beef; sauté until brown. Then add tomatoes, tomato sauce, and all seasonings except Tabasco sauce. Bring to a boil and simmer, stirring occasionally, for 30 minutes. At end of cooking time add pepperoni and Tabasco sauce.

While the meat sauce is simmering, prepare the mushroom and spinach mixtures.

mushrooms:
In a skillet heat olive oil and lightly sauté mushrooms and garlic for 2–3 minutes. Add remaining ingredients and set aside.

spinach:
Melt butter and sauté onion and garlic until soft. Add spinach and cook 3–4 minutes more. Add seasonings, parsley, and fresh cream.

Preheat oven to 375°F.

Lightly grease a 2-quart casserole with olive oil and pour in 1 cup of the meat sauce. Spread ⅕ of the pasta over it and cover with ⅓ of remaining meat sauce. Then follow with ½ mashed tofu, another ⅕ of the pasta, all the mushrooms, ⅕ of the pasta, all the spinach, ⅕ of the pasta, ⅓ of the meat sauce, the rest of the tofu, and the rest of the pasta, ending with the last ⅓ of the meat sauce.

Bake 40–45 minutes.

Remove from oven and let stand at room temperature 5–6 minutes so the sauce settles, which makes it easier to cut. Serve hot.

GRANDMA MA'S TOFU

This is a Sichuan recipe. A little meat and plenty of tofu are sautéed together with the spicy flavors of Sichuan pepper (*hua-jiau*), red pepper, and fermented black beans. Surprisingly, it has been verified that this famous dish was invented by an elderly lady who cooked lunches for workers at the end of the last century and who was nicknamed Grandma Ma.

(serves 4–6)

"A"
1 Tbsp each soy sauce and saké
½ lb ground beef
1 tsp finely chopped fresh ginger root
1 clove garlic, finely chopped
2 Tbsps Chinese soup stock (see p. 24)

"B"
1 Tbsp Chinese fermented black beans, chopped

1 Tbsp Sichuan pepper (*hua-jiau*) pods, chopped with knife (1 tsp powdered)
2 red peppers, seeded and chopped
3 Tbsps soy sauce
2 Tbsps saké

3 Tbsps vegetable oil
1 cake "cotton" tofu, drained by Method I and cut into ½-inch cubes

Mix "A" ingredients well. Mix "B" ingredients. Heat a wok over high heat until smoky. Add oil and again heat until smoky. Stir-fry "A" ingredients over high heat for 1–2 minutes, until beef is browned. Pour "B" mixture over beef and continue to stir-fry over high heat until oil is separated from mixture and turns red (from the red pepper). Add tofu. Cook for 2–3 minutes, stirring lightly from the bottom of the wok, until tofu is thoroughly heated. Serve hot.

STIR-FRIED TOFU, BEEF, AND TOMATO

(color plate 9)

This Taiwanese dish resembles Western cooking in the way the onions are sautéed first. It just might be descended from a Dutch or Portuguese visit at some early date.

(serves 6)

marinade:
1 clove garlic, finely
  chopped
1 tsp finely grated fresh
  ginger root
1 Tbsp saké
1 Tbsp soy sauce
1 tsp cornstarch

½ lb beef rump, sliced
  ¼-inch thick and cut into
  2-inch pieces
5 Tbsps vegetable oil
1 cup sliced onion

1 lb ripe tomatoes, peeled,
  seeded, and chopped
1 cake tofu, drained by
  Method II and mashed
½ cup Chinese soup stock
  (see p. 24)
¼ cup saké
1½ tsps salt
¼ tsp pepper
1 tsp cornstarch dissolved in
  2 Tbsps water
1 large egg, well beaten

Mix marinade ingredients and marinate beef for 10 minutes.

Heat oil to 200°F in a wok or frying pan. Dip beef pieces into the hot oil for 1 minute then drain on a rack. Pour all but 3 Tbsps oil from the wok, then sauté onion over medium heat until golden. Add tomato, tofu, and beef; turn heat to high and stir-fry for 3–4 minutes. Add soup stock, saké, salt, and pepper and bring to a boil. Add cornstarch mixture and cook, stirring, for 1 minute or until thickened. Add the beaten egg so that it spreads evenly and cook another minute.

Serve immediately.

SAUTÉED TOFU AND CRABMEAT
(color plate 12)

This traditional Chinese dish combines delicate, subtle flavors and equally subtle colors and textures. Take care and do not let the tofu loose its shape.

(serves 6)

½ cake tofu, drained by Method I, cut in half lengthwise then into 1-inch slices
salt
5–6 Tbsps vegetable oil
2 Tbsps finely chopped scallions or chives
1 Tbsp finely chopped fresh ginger root

½ lb fresh or frozen crab legs, cartilage removed but not flaked
½ cup Chinese soup stock (see p. 24)
1 tsp soy sauce
1 tsp salt
½ cup saké
1 Tbsp cornstarch dissolved in 2 Tbsps water

Lightly salt tofu slices and drain again on a kitchen towel for 30 minutes.

Heat 2 Tbsps oil in skillet and sauté tofu until light brown on both sides, adding oil as needed. Remove tofu from skillet and set aside.

In the same skillet, heat 3 Tbsps oil and sauté scallions and ginger for 1 minute. Add crab legs and cook 2 minutes longer. Add soup stock, soy sauce, 1 tsp salt, and saké and bring to a boil. Add tofu slices and heat thoroughly. Remove tofu to a hot serving dish. Stir cornstarch mixture into liquid remaining in pan and cook until thickened. Pour thickened liquid over the tofu slices and serve immediately.

Note: The tofu is removed after heating because it breaks easily. If care is taken to stir gently, the tofu may remain in the skillet while the sauce thickens.

JIA-CHANG TOFU
(color plate 10)

Here fried tofu is sautéed with thinly sliced pork and vegetables. An old Chinese friend of mine taught me to add *hua-jiau* to the sauce. This dish is excellent served with rice.

(serves 6)

1 tsp each saké and soy sauce
½ tsp cornstarch
½ lb pork loin, cut into ⅓-inch slices and then into triangular pieces
5 Tbsps vegetable oil
1 cake tofu, drained by Method II and cut same as pork
¼ cup finely chopped scallions or chives
1 tsp finely chopped fresh ginger root
1 clove garlic, finely chopped
2 dried red peppers, cut in half and seeded

5–6 dried *shiitake* mushrooms, reconstituted in warm water for 30 minutes, stems removed, and cut same as pork
1 cup sliced bamboo shoots, cut same as pork

seasonings:
1 Tbsp Sichuan hot bean sauce
4 Tbsps soy sauce
1 tsp salt
1 tsp sugar

2 tsps powdered Sichuan pepper (*hua-jiau*)

Combine saké, soy sauce, and cornstarch and marinate pork for 10 minutes. Heat 3 Tbsps oil in skillet and brown both sides of tofu. Remove from skillet and set aside.

In the same skillet heat 2 Tbsps oil and sauté scallions, ginger, garlic, red pepper, and marinated pork until pork is browned. Add *shiitake* mushrooms and bamboo shoots and sauté another 3–4 minutes. Add seasonings and mix well. Add tofu and cook until heated. Sprinkle with powdered Sichuan pepper and serve immediately.

STIR-FRIED GREEN VEGETABLES AND TOFU
(color plate 14)

Vegetables should never be overcooked. One of the secrets of Chinese cooking is to cook all vegetables fast for a very short time.

(serves 6)

½ cup vegetable oil
1 cake tofu, drained by
   Method III and cut into
   1–2-inch pieces (rec-
   tangles, triangles, or
   squares)
1 tsp salt
½ lb spinach or mustard
   greens, cut into 2-inch
   lengths

1 Tbsp finely chopped
   scallions or chives
1 clove garlic, finely
   chopped
1 Tbsp soy sauce
1 tsp salt
2 Tbsps saké

Heat the vegetable oil in a skillet. Lightly brown both sides of the tofu, a layer at a time, and drain on paper towels. Pour off all but ¼ cup oil.

Reheat oil and add 1 tsp salt. Add the leaf vegetables and stir-fry for 1 minute over high heat. Remove greens to colander, leaving about 1 Tbsp oil in skillet.

Reheat oil in skillet and add scallion, garlic, and tofu. Stir-fry for 2–3 minutes over medium heat. Add the soy sauce, salt, and saké and stir-fry for 1 minute over high heat; return the greens to the skillet and mix quickly. Serve immediately.

CHINESE DEEP-FRIED TOFU
(color plate 13)

Sichuan pepper (*hua-jiau*) is a favorite seasoning used in Sichuan-style Chinese cooking. It can be obtained in most Chinese food stores, but, if unavailable, coarsely ground black pepper can be substituted.

(serves 4–6)

1 cake tofu, drained by
   Method I and cut into
   quarters
⅓ cup flour
vegetable oil for deep-frying

1 tsp powdered Sichuan
   pepper (*hua-jiau*) or
   coarsely ground black
   pepper
1 tsp salt

Dredge tofu with flour. Heat oil to medium temperature (340°F) and fry 4–5 pieces at a time until browned; drain on paper towels. When all are fried, sprinkle with Sichuan pepper and salt. Serve hot.

HEAVENLY TOFU
(color plate 11)

This recipe comes from North China, and its name in Chinese means "favorite." It is best served with vinegar-soy sauce.

(serves 6)

1 cake tofu, drained by Method II
4–5 ounces white-fleshed fish
4–5 ounces shrimp, shelled and deveined
2 Tbsps saké
1 tsp salt
1 tsp cornstarch
1 egg white
4 Tbsps vegetable oil
½ tsp salt
1 lb leaf vegetables (spinach, mustard greens, or but-
terhead lettuce), washed and excess water shaken off, not dried

vinegar-soy sauce:
1 Tbsp finely chopped scallions or chives
3 Tbsps rice vinegar
1 Tbsp sesame oil
2 Tbsps saké
2 Tbsps soy sauce

Put first seven ingredients into processor or blender and process until smooth. Wet hands and mold tofu mixture into a dome shape on an oiled plate. Steam for 20 minutes.

Meanwhile heat 4 Tbsps oil in large frying pan or wok over high heat. Add ½ tsp salt and leaf vegetable and cook, covered, 10 seconds. Stir well and cook, covered, another 10 seconds. Drain greens in colander or on rack. The combination of hot oil and steam cooks the greens very quickly.

Blend sauce ingredients. Serve tofu surrounded by greens with sauce in a separate dish.

STEAMED SEA BREAM WITH KENCHIN FILLING

(color plate 8)

Sea bream (*tai* in Japanese) is a silver-pink fish that is given a special significance in Japan. Traditionally a symbol of happiness and prosperity, it is part of the food served at festive or auspicious occasions such as celebrations at New Years or weddings. It is an interesting fish, one that appeals almost as much to the visual senses as to the palate.

There are numerous recipes for *tai*, and many are peculiar to certain regions. The one here is a speciality of the Kanazawa district. It calls for a carefully prepared tofu stuffing that combines well with the delicate flavor of the white meat of this fish.

(serves 6–8)

2–3-lb sea bream (*tai*), scaled
1 tsp salt

kenchin filling:
3 Tbsps vegetable oil
½ cup finely chopped lotus
  root
½ cup shredded burdock
  root (*gobō*)
½ small carrot, finely
  chopped
2 *shiitake* mushrooms,
  reconstituted in warm
  water for 30 minutes,

stems removed, and thinly
  sliced
2 cups *dashi* (see p. 24)
⅓ cup saké
1 Tbsp soy sauce
2 tsps salt
½ tsp sugar
1 ½ cups *okara*
3 Tbsps vinegar
10 ginkgo nuts

vinegar-soy sauce:
½ cup vinegar
2 Tbsps soy sauce
⅓ cup *dashi* or to taste (see
  p. 24)

Cut the fish along the dorsal fin. Do not cut the belly. Loosen the sides from the bones with a knife. Then, using scissors, cut the bone at the head and tail joints and remove carefully.

Make a slanting cut below the gill flap and remove the entrails.

Wash under running water and wipe dry. Sprinkle with 1 tsp salt and let stand for ½ hour.

Meanwhile, prepare the filling. Heat oil in pan over medium heat and stir-fry the lotus root, burdock, carrot, and *shiitake* mushrooms for 3–4 minutes. Add *dashi*, saké, soy sauce, salt, and sugar. Stir in *okara* and cook, stirring constantly, for 20 minutes or until you can see the bottom of the pan while stirring.

Stir in vinegar and ginkgo nuts. Remove from heat and let cool.

Preheat oven to 375°F.

Stuff the sea bream with the cooled *kenchin* filling.

Pour hot water into a deep baking dish and place an oiled rack over the baking dish so it is about ½ inch above the surface of the water. Place fish on rack. Cover with a heavy-duty aluminum foil tent, being careful not to let foil touch the fish. Bake for 1 hour. The fish should not be browned.

Mix vinegar and soy sauce. Taste and thin with *dashi* as desired while the fish is cooking.

Transfer fish to heated platter and serve with vinegar-soy sauce, which may be poured on fish to taste, in a separate bowl.

SUKIYAKI
(color plate 8)

Sukiyaki, perhaps in name alone the best known of all Japanese dishes outside Japan, is unique among meat-based dishes in that it conforms to traditional methods of preparation, cooking, and serving, whereas other meat dishes are patterned after Western cuisine. This is perhaps not so strange when one considers that beef played almost no part in the Japanese diet until a century ago.

Sukiyaki is cooked at the table in a heavy iron skillet. The almost paper-thin slices of beef constitute only a small part of this dish, whose ingredients also include a wide assortment of vegetables and grilled tofu. This fact means that *sukiyaki* can be eaten the year round, the selection of the ingredients mirroring the changes in the seasons. Grilled tofu is used because it contains less water than conventional "cotton" and "silk" tofu and thus is harder and absorbs less of the pan juices while keeping its unique tofu flavor.

The fact that *sukiyaki* is not served on individual dishes also adds to its appeal. Diners help themselves directly from the skillet, and this helps to create the friendly, cozy atmosphere that characterizes a *sukiyaki* meal.

(serves 6)

seasoning sauce:
1 cup soybeans, rinsed
3×7-inch sheet *kobu* kelp,
   wiped lightly with a damp
   cloth
2 cups water
1¼ cups soy sauce
1¼ cups mirin
¼ cup sugar

3–4 ounces suet
2 lbs thinly sliced sirloin beef
3 leeks, cut into diagonal
   slices

1 lb chrysanthemum leaves
   (*shungiku*)
1 medium bamboo shoot,
   cut into thin slices
12 fresh small *matsutake* or
   shiitake mushrooms
½ lb *shirataki* (*konnyaku*
   noodles), blanched for 1–2
   minutes and drained
1 cake grilled tofu (*yaki-
   dofu*), cut into 16 pieces
6 eggs

Soak soybeans and *kobu* kelp in water for about 1 day. Strain.

Combine 1 cup soybean-*kobu* stock with soy sauce, mirin, and sugar. Bring to a boil and skim.

At the table, heat pan over medium heat and melt suet. Add several slices of beef. When the beef starts sizzling, quickly pour in seasoning sauce and braise over medium heat. Remove beef, leaving liquid in the pan. Add leek, then the other vegetables, *shirataki*, tofu, and meat. As much as possible avoid mixing the various ingredients in the pan. Add more seasoning sauce as needed.

Serve with a beaten egg in each dipping bowl. Dip the hot ingredients in the egg as you eat them.

CHILLED TOFU
Hiyayakko   (color plate 19)

Chilled tofu is the ideal dish to eat on sultry summer days and is extremely popular with Japanese of all ages in the hot months of the year. Neatly cut, chilled, and served in a frosted glass bowl, chilled tofu is aesthetically pleasing and both looks and tastes cool and refreshing. Prepared simply without elaborate trimmings, it is said to be the best way of appreciating the delicate flavor of tofu. The excellence of the flavor therefore depends heavily upon the quality and the freshness of the tofu used.

The traditional flavor garnishes are used in this recipe, but do not hesitate to be adventurous with your garnishes (see Chilled Tofu with Four Chinese Sauces, page 53).

(serves 6)

1 ½ cakes "cotton" tofu, rinsed carefully in a bowl of cold water and cut into 24 pieces

seasoning:
soy sauce

¼ cup thinly sliced leek
3 Tbsps finely grated fresh ginger root
⅓ cup lightly packed dried bonito shavings (**katsuobushi**; optional)

Put tofu cubes into a glass bowl filled with ice water.

Pour a little soy sauce in individual small dishes and mix in leek, ginger, and bonito shavings to taste. Dip tofu into sauce.

SIMMERING TOFU
Yudōfu   (color plate 18)

This, the opposite of Chilled Tofu (preceding), is the other major traditional way tofu is eaten in Japan. Here, also, the tofu is garnished, but only so that its natural flavor can speak more clearly. There are few dishes as direct and simple as this. A winter dish.

(serves 6)

3×7-inch sheet *kobu* kelp, wiped lightly with a damp cloth
3–4 cups warm water
1 or 2 cakes tofu, rinsed carefully in a bowl of cold water and cut into 24 cubes

dip:
soy sauce
1 scallion, finely chopped
3 Tbsps finely grated fresh ginger root
1 lemon, cut into 6 wedges

Combine *kobu*, water, and ½ of tofu in a saucepan and bring just to a boil. Reduce heat and simmer only until tofu is heated thoroughly. Cook remaining half of tofu as required. Do not overcook. Serve hot.

Each diner makes his own dip by pouring a little soy sauce into a small plate and mixing it with scallion, ginger, and lemon juice to taste. The tofu is dipped into the soy sauce mixture as it is eaten. Feel free to invent your own dips for this dish.

DEEP-FRIED TOFU
Agedashi-Dōfu   (color plate 15)

This dish is representative of Japanese home cooking. Tofu is deep-fried in a sesame-flavored oil then topped with a simple sauce and a piquant garnish. It should be cooked quickly and served hot.

(serves 4)

sauce:
2 cups *dashi* (see p. 24)
¼ cup saké
3 Tbsps soy sauce
3 Tbsps sugar
⅛ tsp salt

vegetable oil for deep-frying:
  1 part sesame oil, 10 parts
    vegetable oil
1 cake tofu, drained by
  Method I and cut into
  quarters
approximately ⅓ cup flour

momiji-oroshi:
2½-inch slice daikon radish
2–3 dried red peppers,
  seeded

Combine sauce ingredients in a small saucepan, bring to a simmer, and keep warm.

Heat ample oil for deep-frying to medium temperature (340°F).

Dredge tofu with flour and fry 2 pieces at a time until golden, about 4 minutes. (Do not fry too many at once because the action of the hot oil on the water in the tofu may cause the oil to overflow.) Turn over carefully and fry 3 more minutes. Oil must be gently stirred during frying to keep its temperature even.

Place one piece of fried tofu on each medium-sized prewarmed dish. Pour hot sauce over each piece and garnish with *momiji-oroshi*.

Momiji-oroshi ("grated red maple") is a perfect complement to many Japanese dishes. If daikon is unavailable, finely slice an onion and soak it for 5 minutes in cold water. Drain and sprinkle with cayenne or Tabasco sauce and a few drops of lemon or lime juice.

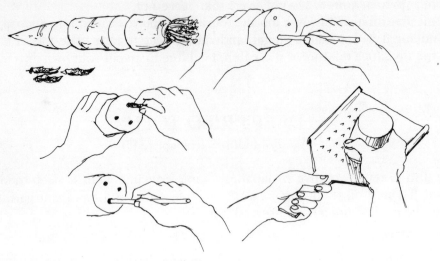

Make 2–3 holes in daikon radish with a chopstick; insert dried red peppers into holes with the chopstick and grate daikon finely.

SCRAMBLED TOFU
Iri-Dōfu   (color plate 15)

Here is a convenient dish to make when faced with unexpected guests. It is home cooking, informal and delicious, and all kinds of other vegetables can be added, especially root vegetables. Basically it is vegetarian fare and part of Buddhist temple cooking.

(serves 6)

2–3 Tbsps vegetable oil
1 Tbsp sesame oil (optional)
1 medium carrot, cut into julienne strips
1 medium green pepper, cut into julienne strips
1/4 lb snow peas
2 *shiitake* mushrooms, reconstituted in warm water for 30 minutes, stems removed, and thinly sliced

1 sheet thin deep-fried tofu (*abura-age*), rinsed quickly with boiling water to remove excess oil, blotted dry, cut in half lengthwise then into julienne strips crosswise
1/2 cake tofu, drained by Method II

seasoning:
3 Tbsps soy sauce
1/2 tsp salt
2 Tbsps saké

Heat oils in a pan and sauté carrot, green pepper, snow peas, *shiitake* mushrooms, and *abura-age* for 4–5 minutes over medium heat. Add the tofu, crushing it with a wooden spatula. Continue sautéing for another 3–4 minutes, or until the tofu becomes crumbly and watery looking. Add soy sauce, salt, and saké and cook for an additional 2–3 minutes or until vegetables soften. The tofu should still be moist.

Note: If you like, you can add a well-beaten egg with the soy sauce and other seasonings. The egg absorbs the liquid, so the result will be stiffer.

VEGETABLES WITH WHITE DRESSING

Traditionally this is a winter dish, and it is often served at the Doll Festival in early March.

Carrots, thin deep-fried tofu, and *konnyaku* are the standard ingredients in this recipe, but, thinking deep-fried tofu and *konnyaku* might be difficult to obtain in some cases, I tried Westernizing this dish a little by using carrots and green beans instead, with good results.

(serves 4–6)

stock for cooking carrots:	dressing:
⅔ cup *dashi* (see p. 24)	½ cake tofu
1 Tbsp saké	2 Tbsps white sesame seeds
1 tsp salt	½ cup *dashi* (see p. 24)
1 Tbsp sugar	1 tsp salt
1 Tbsp soy sauce	1 Tbsp sugar
	1 tsp soy sauce
1 carrot, cut into julienne strips	
	½ lb green beans, cut into julienne strips and parboiled

Bring *dashi*, saké, salt, sugar, and soy sauce to a boil in a small saucepan. Add carrot strips and cook until done and liquid is almost gone. Drain.

Bring ample amount of water to a boil. Add tofu and boil 3 minutes. Drain, then wrap in cheesecloth and squeeze out as much liquid as possible. Unwrap and mash.

Toast sesame seeds in dry frying pan over low heat until one or two seeds pop. Grind with mortar and pestle until a flaky paste is formed. Put ground sesame seeds and all other ingredients for the dressing in a food processor or blender and process until smooth.

Combine carrots, string beans, and dressing and mix well.

Serve at room temperature in individual bowls.

RICE WITH DEEP-FRIED TOFU
Abura-Age Gohan

It is most important that freshly cooked, piping hot rice be used for this recipe. You will find that no additional condiments or spices are necessary and that the combined aroma of the dried bonito shavings and the tofu alone will whet your appetite.

(serves 6)

3 sheets thin deep-fried tofu (*abura-age*), rinsed quickly with boiling water to remove excess oil, blotted dry, cut in half lengthwise then into julienne strips crosswise
1 cup water

1 cup lightly packed dried bonito shavings (*katsuo-bushi*)
⅓ cup soy sauce
⅓ cup saké
4–5 cups hot, freshly cooked rice

Combine all ingredients except rice, and cook, covered, over medium-low heat for 15 minutes. Uncover and continue to cook for 4–5 more minutes, or until all liquid is gone.

Gently mix with piping hot rice and serve.

Salads

SPINACH SALAD

Salad dressings made with tofu are a traditional part of Japanese cuisine. This creamy tofu dressing gives freshness and originality to the highly popular American spinach salad.

(serves 6)

dressing:
- 3 Tbsps sugar
- 1 ½ tsps salt
- ¼ tsp pepper
- ½ cup vegetable oil
- ¼ cup vinegar
- ½ cake "silk" tofu, drained by Method I and lightly squeezed in cheesecloth

salad:
- 1 lb young spinach, washed, dried thoroughly, and torn into bite-sized pieces
- 1 stalk celery, diced
- ½ head iceberg lettuce, torn into bite-sized pieces
- 3–4 slices crisp-fried bacon, crumbled

Blend all dressing ingredients except tofu with a wire whisk. Add tofu and whisk until smooth.

Add dressing to spinach and celery and toss lightly. Add lettuce and bacon and retoss. Serve immediately.

SNOW WHITE SALAD

This is an extremely nutritious salad that appeals to the eye as much as to the palate. The thin slices of cauliflower give the dish the appearance of being frosted with snow.

(serves 6)

salad:
lemon juice
½ lb raw cauliflower
   flowerets, thinly sliced
¼ cup thinly sliced
   mushrooms

dressing:
3 Tbsps lemon juice

⅓ cup olive oil
1 ½ tsps salt
pepper to taste
1 Tbsp egg white, slightly
   beaten
¼ cake tofu, drained by
   Method II and mashed
½ cup cottage cheese

Sprinkle a little lemon juice on the cauliflower and mushroom slices and set aside.

Put the lemon juice, olive oil, salt, and pepper into a mixing bowl and add the egg white gradually while beating. Stir in the mashed tofu and cottage cheese, then add the prepared vegetables and mix well.

RED CABBAGE AND BLUE CHEESE SALAD
(color plate 22)

One theory states that twelve hundred years ago tofu was first made in China as an imitation of the cheese eaten by Mongolian nomads. Here these distant cousins—tofu and cheese—are combined. Further, the flavor of French dressing with tofu resembles feta cheese. Your favorite cheese may be used instead of the blue.

(serves 4–6)

salad:
1/2 head red cabbage, shredded
1/4 cup vinegar
1 tsp salt

dressing:
4 ounces blue cheese, crumbled

1/4 cake tofu, drained by Method III and cut into 1/2-inch cubes
1/3 cup French dressing
1 clove garlic, crushed
1/4 tsp caraway seeds

Mix red cabbage, vinegar, and salt and set aside for 10–15 minutes to make the cabbage a fresh brilliant purple. Squeeze out moisture.

Combine blue cheese, tofu, French dressing, garlic, and caraway seeds. Add cabbage and mix well. Cover the bowl with plastic wrap and chill before serving.

INDIAN YOGHURT SALAD

A refreshing yoghurt salad often accompanies curry in India. Here I have added tofu as well. The bland flavor of the tofu and yoghurt complements the spicy curry. Try this salad the next time you have a curry dinner.

(serves 6)

salad:
1 large onion, thinly sliced, soaked in water to remove harsh flavor, and drained
3 cucumbers, cut into 1/4-inch slices
3 large tomatoes, cut into 1/4-inch slices

dressing:
1/2 cake tofu, drained by Method II and mashed
1 cup yoghurt
2 tsps finely grated fresh ginger root
2 cloves garlic, finely chopped
2 tsps salt
dash pepper

Drain and pat dry the onion slices and arrange attractively with the cucumbers and tomatoes on a plate or in a salad bowl. Mix all dressing ingredients well and pour over the vegetables.

RICE SALAD

The perfect Oriental combination of rice and tofu is adjusted here to suit the Mediterranean palate. The broiled eggplant adds a special fragrance to this salad.

(serves 6)

1 medium eggplant

dressing:
3 Tbsps lemon juice
⅓ cup olive oil
salt and pepper to taste
¼ cup chopped fresh basil

salad:
8-ounce can whole kernel
   corn, drained
8 ounces mushrooms, sliced
¼ cup shredded pimiento
¼ cup finely chopped
   onion, soaked in water to

remove harsh flavor and
   drained
2 Tbsps finely chopped
   chives
½ cup finely chopped green
   pepper
¼ cup chopped black olives
½ cake tofu, drained by
   Method II and cut into
   ½-inch cubes
1 ½ cups cooked rice

lettuce to cover bottom of
   salad bowl

Broil eggplant 2 inches from heat, turning frequently, until skin bubbles and chars. Peel and cut into ½-inch cubes.

Combine all dressing ingredients, mixing well.

Mix all salad ingredients, including eggplant, adding rice last. Toss with dressing and chill.

Serve on bed of lettuce.

DEEP-FRIED TOFU SALAD WITH MUSTARD DRESSING

You will find other recipes calling for deep-fried tofu in this book, some taken from Chinese and some from Japanese style cooking. I have included this recipe because I wanted to illustrate how extremely versatile tofu is and the great variety of ways in which it can be enjoyed, depending on the coatings and seasonings used.

Here I have tried using deep-fried tofu in combination with a mustard dressing. The tofu is cut in fairly small squares, dredged in cornmeal, and deep-fried. Not only does the use of cornmeal enhance the flavor of the tofu, it gives the tofu a firm, crisp outer coat and a nice, chewy bite. The mustard with crushed seeds used for the dressing complements the flavor of the tofu admirably. Care should be taken that the mustard dressing is well blended and smooth. The dish is served and eaten while the tofu is piping hot.

(serves 6)

vegetable oil for deep-frying
5–6 lettuce leaves

dressing:
½ cup vegetable oil
2 Tbsps wine vinegar
1 Tbsp mustard with crushed seeds (*moutarde de
   meaux*)

½ tsp Worcestershire sauce
1 tsp salt
dash pepper

1 cake tofu, drained by
   Method II and cut into
   1 × 1 × ½-inch pieces
½ cup or more cornmeal

Heat oil to medium temperature (340°F).

Line salad bowl with lettuce leaves. Set aside.

Combine all mustard dressing ingredients and set aside. Dredge tofu in cornmeal. Fry ⅓ of it at a time, stirring gently to prevent sticking, for 2–3 minutes, or until golden-brown. As each batch is completed, drain on paper towels and keep warm. When all are done, mix tofu quickly with the dressing. Pour tofu and dressing into the lettuce-lined salad bowl and serve.

Note: Do not deep-fry too much tofu at once because the vigorous action of the oil on the moist tofu may cause hot oil to overflow.

TOFU-TOMATO SALAD IN AVOCADO BOATS

(serves 6)

3 avocados

dressing:
¼ cake tofu, drained by
   Method II and mashed
⅓ cup mayonnaise
¼ cup sour cream
2 Tbsps finely chopped
   onion
2 tsps lemon juice

½ tsp salt
dash pepper

2 medium tomatoes, peeled,
   seeded, and cut into
   ½-inch pieces
¼ cake tofu, drained by
   Method II and cut into
   ½-inch cubes

Cut the avocados in half lengthwise and remove the seeds. Using a spoon, scoop out the pulp to within ½ inch of the shell and set aside. Dice pulp into ½-inch pieces.

   Blend all dressing ingredients with a wire whisk. Add the tomatoes, avocado, and tofu to the dressing and spoon into avocado shells. Chill and serve.

   The mixture can also be served directly on lettuce, sprinkled with paprika.

MEDITERRANEAN SALAD

Cold cooked vegetables are often served as hors d'oeuvres in Western cuisine. This unusual combination of tofu, eggplant, and asparagus flavored with slivers of garlic, chilled, and served with a rich mayonnaise and cream sauce is a bright and delicious dish. Though tofu is simply added to this classical recipe, I feel that it enhances the contrasts of flavors and textures and adds interest. It is likely that if tofu had been made in the Mediterranean area, it would have been included.

(serves 6–8)

2 medium eggplants, cut in
 half lengthwise
2 tsps salt
4–5 cloves garlic, sliced
1/2–1 cup olive oil
pepper to taste
1 lb asparagus

mayonnaise sauce:
1 1/2 cups mayonnaise
1 tsp sugar
1/2 cup heavy cream
2 Tbsps lemon juice

1 cake "silk" tofu, drained
 by Method I and chilled

Sprinkle eggplant halves with 2 tsps salt and set aside for 1/2 hour. Rinse to remove excess salt and squeeze out water.

Sauté garlic in 3 Tbsps olive oil for 2–3 minutes over medium-low heat until light brown in color, taking care not to burn. Remove and drain on paper towel.

Add remaining olive oil to pan and fry eggplant slices until both sides are light brown. Remove and drain on paper towels. Sprinkle with pepper and chill.

Prepare asparagus by breaking off the hard bottom (about 2 inches) of the stem and peeling the stem up to the tip. Boil gently until barely tender—about 3–4 minutes. Plunge into cold water, drain, and pat dry. Chill.

Mix ingredients for mayonnaise sauce.

Slice the tofu cake about 1/2-inch thick and arrange in a continuous layer on a long serving platter. Place a layer of fried eggplant on top of the tofu and a layer of asparagus on top of the eggplant. Sprinkle with sautéed garlic slices. Serve the mayonnaise sauce separately.

garlic
asparagus
eggplant
tofu

QUICK FRUIT SALAD

Fruit and tofu make an excellent combination. Here it is used in a semisweet salad with a refreshing yoghurt dressing (see also Fruit Compote, page 145). Any combination of fresh or canned fruit may be used.

(serves 6)

dressing:
1 cup yoghurt
½ cake "silk" tofu, drained
    by Method II and mashed
⅓ cup juice from canned
    fruit

½ cup honey
1 Tbsp lemon juice
½ tsp poppy seeds
1 tsp salt
¼ tsp pepper

salad:
½ lb strawberries
1 apple
1 orange
1 avocado
2 cups any canned fruit

} cut into bite-sized pieces
(save juice for dressing)

½ cake "silk" tofu, drained by Method I and cut into ½-inch cubes
¼ cup chopped walnuts

Combine dressing ingredients and pour over fruits and tofu. Chill for 1 hour. Serve in individual serving bowls, sprinkled with chopped walnuts.

APPLE AND CELERY SALAD

(color plate 20)

(serves 4–6)

dressing:
⅓ cup heavy cream,
    whipped
½ cup mayonnaise
1 Tbsp sugar
½ tsp salt
¼ tsp white pepper

salad:
1 medium apple, cut into
    ½×½×¼-inch pieces

1 medium red onion,
    chopped
1 stalk celery, cut into
    ½-inch pieces
½ cake "silk" tofu, drained
    by Method I and cut into
    ½-inch cubes
⅓ cup chopped walnuts

Prepare dressing by combining whipped cream with mayonnaise, sugar, salt, and white pepper.

Add dressing to apple, red onion, and celery and toss thoroughly. Add tofu and mix carefully.

Place in salad bowl, sprinkle with chopped walnuts, and serve.

SPRING GARDEN SALAD
(color plate 21)

This recipe is reminiscent of one of the basic categories of Japanese cuisine, *sunomono*, comprising fish, or meat, or vegetables in a piquant, slightly sweetened vinegar dressing. This salad is made with a lot of dressing and, I would like to stress, should be served with it.

(serves 6)

salad:
½ cake tofu, cut into
  ½-inch cubes
8 ounces fresh cooked or
  frozen crab legs, cartilage
  removed but not flaked
¼ lb *enokitake* mushrooms,
  thick base removed
1 cucumber, halved lengthwise, seeded, and cut into
  julienne strips
1 carrot, cut into julienne
  strips
¼ lb bean sprouts, parboiled and drained well

2 small green peppers, cut
  into julienne strips
1 tomato, peeled, seeded,
  and cut into ½-inch
  pieces

dressing:
⅔ cup vinegar
1 Tbsp sesame oil
1 Tbsp soy sauce
2 tsps salt
⅛ tsp pepper
¼ cup sugar

Combine salad ingredients in a large mixing bowl.

Mix all dressing ingredients well, pour over salad, and toss.

Transfer to individual salad bowls with an ample portion of dressing.

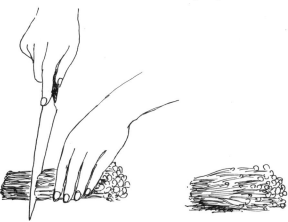

PAO-CAI SALAD

(color plate 21)

Freshly made pickles are popular in both China and Japan. This salad is ready for eating after marinating overnight, but the flavor is greatly improved if it can be left to marinate for 2 or 3 days. Try using it as a relish with sandwiches.

(serves 6)

salad:
1/4 medium daikon radish, cut into 1/2 × 2-inch pieces, sprinkled with salt and left for 30 minutes
1 carrot, cut same as daikon
2 small green peppers, cut into julienne strips
1/2 cucumber, sliced thinly on the diagonal
1 celery stalk, cut into 3/4-inch rectangles
5–6 cabbage leaves, cut into 3/4-inch rectangles

dressing:
1 clove garlic, sliced
1-inch knob fresh ginger root, sliced
1/4 cup vegetable oil
1 tsp vinegar
1 tsp coarsely ground pepper

2–3 Tbsps vegetable oil (for sautéing tofu)
tofu

Combine all salad and dressing ingredients except tofu and oil for sautéing and chill overnight.

Heat 2–3 Tbsps oil in skillet and sauté tofu until lightly browned. Drain and cool on paper towels.

Mix with marinated vegetables and serve.

TOFU SALAD

(serves 4)

1 small red onion, thinly sliced

dressing:
1/3 cup vinegar
2 Tbsps vegetable oil

1/2 tsp salt
1 tsp soy sauce

1 cake "silk" tofu, drained by Method I

Rinse sliced onion in cold water and pat dry.

Blend the dressing ingredients.

Cut the tofu into four equal squares. Place each square in an individual bowl and top with onions. Pour on the dressing and serve.

Sauces, Dips, and Spreads

FRENCH DRESSING

I find that adding mashed tofu to a standard French dressing gives it a creamier flavor. I think this dressing is a good example of how, with clever additions and adaptations, some dishes act as bridges between Oriental and Western cooking. I like to experiment with it, so I do not limit myself to using it only with green salads. Try adding a little mustard to this recipe and use it with potato salad, or try combining it with a bit of ground sesame (or sesame oil) and soy sauce for a more Oriental touch.

(makes 2 cups)

½ cake tofu, drained by Method II and mashed	1 Tbsp lemon juice
⅔ cup olive oil	2 tsps salt
⅓ cup vinegar	¼ tsp pepper
	⅛ tsp sugar

Blend all ingredients. The dressing can be blended until it is homogeneous and creamy, or you can stop blending while the tofu is still in tiny lumps—both styles are delicious.

MAYONNAISE

(makes 2 cups)

yolks from 2 3-minute boil- ed eggs	1 cup vegetable oil
1 tsp powdered mustard	3 Tbsps vinegar
½ cake "cotton" tofu, drained by Method III	1 tsp salt
	pinch sugar

In a food processor, process egg yolks, mustard, and tofu until smooth and liquid. Add oil 1 Tbsp at a time while processing until half the oil is used, then add 2 Tbsps at a time. Season to taste with vinegar, salt, and sugar.

If making by hand with a wire whisk, follow the same procedure, except add oil 1 tsp at a time until half is used, then add 1 Tbsp at a time.

Dip:
Combine mayonnaise, 1 cup sour cream, 2 Tbsps finely chopped walnuts, 2 Tbsps chopped chives, then anything you like, finely chopped.

WHITE TOFU DRESSING

This classic Japanese dressing can be used on almost anything. Do not hesitate to make any additions you like.

(makes 1 cup)

½ cake tofu, drained by Method I	1 tsp salt
2 Tbsps white sesame seeds	1 Tbsp sugar
½ cup *dashi* (see p. 24)	1 tsp soy sauce
	1 Tbsp *miso*

Combine all ingredients.

GARLIC SPREAD

Marvelous on French bread.

(makes ½ cup)

1 bulb garlic
4 Tbsps butter
½ cake tofu, drained by
    Method II
1–3 anchovy fillets
½ tsp salt

Peel garlic cloves and place in small saucepan with butter. Cook, uncovered, on lowest heat until garlic cloves are soft. Do not let garlic brown, because it gets bitter. Cool.

Blend all ingredients in a blender or food processor. Or, mash garlic cloves and tofu very well and blend everything with a wire whisk.

Refrigerate. Keeps 2 days.

HORSERADISH-TOFU DIP

(approximately 1 ¼ cups)

⅓ cup heavy cream, chilled
3 Tbsps lemon juice
½ tsp salt

3 Tbsps grated fresh
    horseradish (or prepared
    horseradish)
¼ cake "silk" tofu, drained
    by Method I and mashed

Whip cream until it holds soft peaks. Add remaining ingredients slowly, beating constantly, until smooth. Refrigerate.

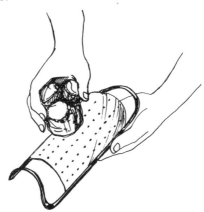

SOYBEAN AND MISO DIP

This piquant dip uses whole soybeans, the mama and papa of both tofu and miso, for a texture and flavor emphasis. The addition of tofu here makes the dip gentler in flavor, but tofu is not necessary.

(makes 2 cups)

1 cup dried soybeans	3 Tbsps saké
2 Tbsps vegetable oil	1 Tbsp sugar
1 Tbsp sesame oil	1 Tbsp toasted white sesame
1 cup red *miso*	seeds
½ cake "cotton" tofu	
(optional)	

Parch soybeans in dry frying pan over medium heat until lightly spotted. Cool.
   Place oils in a saucepan over medium heat, add *miso*, and sauté, stirring constantly, until all oil is absorbed and *miso* takes on a sheen. Add tofu (optional) and sauté until well blended. Add saké and sugar and sauté, while blending, for 2–3 minutes. Mix in sesame seeds and parched soybeans. Keeps indefinitely if tofu is not used.

Breakfast and Lunch

PROTEIN PUNCH

A breakfast drink or snack.

>   (serves 1)

>>   ½ cup soy milk
>>   ½ cup fruit juice

Simply mix chilled soy milk and juice.

HOT TOFU MILK

A drink with body, just right for getting you going on those chilly mornings, and ideal for the sleepy-head who never leaves him- or herself time for a proper breakfast.

>   (serves 1)

>>   ¼ cake "silk" tofu, drained   1 cup milk
>>   by Method I and cut into   1 Tbsp butter
>>   ½-inch cubes   dash salt

Warm all ingredients and serve.

Variation: Omit salt, and add honey and a dash of nutmeg.

TOFU FRUIT CUP

"Silk" tofu is fine-textured and so very like a light egg custard that it is a natural in a combination of this sort. This is one of the recipes that might liberate tofu from the rather conservative image it has held up to now and alert the culinary world to the versatility of this extremely nutritious food.

(serves 2–4)

½ cake "silk" tofu, drained by Method I and cut into ½-inch cubes
½ lb strawberries, sliced

1 banana, sliced
about ½ cup honey
1 Tbsp lemon juice

Place tofu in a bowl, cover with sliced strawberries and banana; top with mixture of honey and lemon juice.

Variations:
Sprinkle with a crunchy cereal.
Add apricot or other jam.
Substitute yoghurt and jam for fresh fruit.

TOFU SCRAMBLED EGGS

(serves 4)

4 large eggs
2 tsps salt
⅛ tsp nutmeg
pepper to taste

3 Tbsps butter
½ cake tofu, drained by Method II and mashed

Beat eggs in a bowl with salt, nutmeg, and pepper to taste. Melt butter in frying pan over medium heat. Add tofu and scramble until crumbly. Whey starts to show in 1 minute, but further scrambling reduces it. Add egg mixture and proceed as for scrambled eggs. Serve hot.

TOFU SPANISH OMELET

When I experimented by adding tofu to a Spanish omelet, I found it blended so well with the vegetables used in the standard recipe that this new variation soon became a firm favorite with everyone who tried it.

(serves 4)

½ cake tofu, drained by Method II and cut into ½-inch cubes	2 medium tomatoes, peeled, seeded, and cut into 1-inch pieces
2 Tbsps flour	salt and pepper to taste
5 Tbsps butter	4 large eggs
1 small onion, sliced	parsley sprigs
1 cup sliced mushrooms	

Preheat oven to 350°F.

Scramble tofu in a frying pan over medium heat until moisture from the tofu is almost gone—about 3–4 minutes. Sprinkle with flour and stir quickly. Remove tofu to a plate and set aside.

Heat 2 Tbsps butter in the same pan and sauté onion until soft but not browned. Add mushrooms and sauté; add tomato and tofu and sauté another 3–4 minutes, then season with salt and pepper to taste. Pour vegetable and tofu mixture into a greased 8-inch pie plate.

Beat eggs, salt, and pepper. Melt remaining butter in frying pan and add egg mixture, stirring quickly to spread over the bottom of the pan. Cook until set. Invert eggs onto the tofu mixture and tuck sides under it.

Reheat 2–3 minutes in oven. Serve hot garnished with parsley.

CREAMED TOFU ON TOAST

(serves 4–6)

sauce:

1 medium onion, finely
    chopped
4 Tbsps butter
2 Tbsps flour
2 cups milk
2 Tbsps dry vermouth
1 tsp salt

dash white pepper

½ cake tofu, drained by
    Method I and cut into
    1-inch slices
hot buttered toast
2 Tbsps finely chopped
    parsley

Sauté onion in butter over low heat until translucent. Add flour and cook, stirring constantly, until well blended—about 1 minute. Over low heat, gradually add milk, stirring until slightly thickened. Add dry vermouth, salt, and pepper and cook slowly for 5–6 minutes. Add tofu and cook for another 5 minutes or until tofu is thoroughly heated. Serve hot on toast. Garnish with chopped parsley.

Baking

TOFU MUFFINS

(10–12 muffins)

1 cup all-purpose flour
½ tsp salt
1 ½ tsps baking powder
½ tsp baking soda
1 cup cornmeal
2 eggs, well beaten

½ cake tofu, drained by
  Method II, squeezed in
  cheesecloth, and pureed
  in processor or blender
½ cup firmly packed brown
  sugar
4 Tbsps melted butter

Preheat oven to 450°F.

Sift together dry ingredients and set aside.

Beat eggs well; add tofu and brown sugar and again beat well. Add sifted dry ingredients and stir lightly and quickly until barely mixed, then fold in melted butter with rubber spatula. Fill well-greased or lined muffin cups ⅔ full. Bake 15–20 minutes, until light gold.

ENGLISH MUFFINS

Here tofu brings a fresh difference to this American breakfast favorite.

(makes 1 dozen)

2 tsps dry yeast
¼ tsp sugar
⅓ cup lukewarm water
1 Tbsp butter
½ cake tofu, drained by
  Method I
1 Tbsp sugar
1 tsp salt

2 cups bread flour
¾ cup cake flour
1 tsp baking powder
2–4 Tbsps cornmeal

Mix yeast, ¼ tsp sugar, and lukewarm water and let stand until frothy.

Melt butter and blend with tofu, sugar, and salt.

Sift together dry ingredients except cornmeal and add yeast and tofu mixtures. Mix until smooth, about 3–4 minutes.

Place dough in oiled bowl, turn once to oil surface of dough, and cover with a damp cloth. Let stand in a warm place until doubled in bulk—about 1–2 hours.

Knead for 1–2 minutes.

Roll out dough to ½-inch thickness and cut into 2 ½-inch rounds with a cutter, glass, or well-washed tuna can.

Spread 1 Tbsp cornmeal on a baking sheet. Place muffins on sheet about 1 inch apart. Sparsely sprinkle tops of muffins with cornmeal. Cover with plastic wrap and let stand in a warm place for 40–60 minutes—until doubled in bulk.

With a pancake turner or spatula, place muffins on a medium-hot griddle or skillet and cook each side 5–6 minutes—until golden.

Best eaten hot. The presence of tofu makes these a little different from conventional English muffins. These muffins will shrink and harden somewhat when cool, but will regain their original size and softness when reheated in foil. Further, these muffin are best eaten as is, without breaking open or toasting. They tend to harden when toasted.

BEATEN BISCUITS

(makes 2 dozen biscuits)

3 cups all-purpose flour	3 Tbsps lard
½ tsp sugar	½ cake "cotton" tofu,
½ tsp salt	drained by Method II
3 Tbsps butter	3 Tbsps melted butter

Heat oven to 325°F.

Sift together flour, sugar, and salt into a bowl.

Add butter and lard and work into dry ingredients with fingertips, as you would pie crust (or use food processor).

Add tofu and mix in by hand.

Place dough on a work surface and knead for 5 minutes. Then take dough and throw it hard against the work surface about 100 times, until texture becomes fine and homogeneous—like your earlobe, as the Japanese say.

Roll out dough to ½-inch thickness and punch out biscuits of about 2-inch diameter with a glass or biscuit cutter.

Place on ungreased baking sheet and prick a number of times with a fork.

Brush with melted butter and bake for 30 minutes. Best eaten hot.

SWEET ROLLS

These are light and totally delicious. Tofu is very successful used in yeast baking, and here is one testament to this fact.

(makes 18–20 rolls)

1 ½ Tbsps dry yeast	3 Tbsps sugar
¼ tsp sugar	2 Tbsps brown sugar
⅓ cup lukewarm water	2 egg yolks
½ cup raisins	1 tsp lemon juice
2 Tbsps rum	1 cake tofu, drained by
4 cups bread flour	Method I and mashed
1 tsp salt	5 Tbsps melted butter
1 Tbsp honey	

Mix yeast, sugar, and lukewarm water and let stand until foamy. Place raisins in rum and let stand while making dough.

In a large bowl, lightly mix remaining ingredients up to and including tofu. Add melted butter, mix briefly, then add yeast. Knead for 15 minutes.

Add rum-soaked raisins (and any rum remaining) and mix well.

Oil a bowl, add dough, and turn once to coat surface. Cover with a damp cloth and let stand in a warm place until doubled in bulk—about 1 ½ hours.

Punch down dough. Divide into 18 pieces and form into balls. Place balls about 2 inches apart on an oiled baking sheet, put in a warm place, and let rise until doubled in bulk—about 30 minutes.

Heat oven to 450°F.

Put rolls in preheated oven and bake for 10–12 minutes, until golden. Serve hot or at room temperature.

Variation 1: Lighter rolls can be made by omitting the rum-soaked raisins and preparing the following ingredients in the same manner as outlined above.

yeast mixture same as	1 egg white
preceding	1 cake tofu, drained by
4 cups bread flour	Method II
2 Tbsps sugar	½ cup milk
½ Tbsp salt	4 Tbsps melted butter

Variation 2: Graham Bread

yeast mixture same as preceding	¼ cup rye flour
4 cups bread flour	2 Tbsps sugar
¼ cup graham flour	½ Tbsp salt
	1 egg white

Prepare in the same manner as Sweet Rolls, but place dough in a 9-inch loaf pan, brush top with melted butter, and bake at 400°F for 35 minutes, or until a hollow sound is made when loaf is tapped.

Variation 3: A variety of coffee cakes can be made by increasing the butter and egg content, with an appropriate small increase in flour. Use the basic Sweet Roll recipe to experiment with and make your own creations.

DILL BREAD

The classic recipe for this marvelous bread uses cottage cheese. Why not substitute tofu? The result is a bread every bit as good as the traditional one but richer and somewhat moister. Makes excellent toast and is delicious with sweet butter.

1 Tbsp dry yeast	½ tsp each baking soda and
2 tsps sugar	baking powder
⅓ cup lukewarm water	1 cake "cotton" tofu, drain-
2½ cups all-purpose flour	ed by Method III
1 large egg	2 tsps dill seed
2 Tbsps melted butter	2 tsps dried dill weed
2 tsps salt	

Mix yeast with sugar and lukewarm water and let stand until foamy.

In a large bowl, place 1 cup flour, add yeast mixture, and mix well. Add egg, melted butter, salt, baking soda, baking powder, tofu, and dill seed and weed and mix well. Then add remaining flour and mix again.

Knead dough about 5 minutes, until smooth. Dredge a bowl with flour, add dough, and cover with a damp cloth. Let stand in a warm place until doubled in bulk—about 1 hour.

Knead dough again for 3 minutes or so. Form a round loaf and place on an ungreased baking sheet (or put in appropriate-sized loaf pan), cover with a damp cloth, and let rise again in a warm place until doubled in bulk.

Heat oven to 375°F.

Place baking sheet (or loaf pan) in oven and bake about 40 minutes or until the loaf sounds hollow when tapped.

CHOUX PASTRY

Tofu is liquefied and used instead of water in making choux pastry. The result is delicious deep-fried.

This pastry may be used for nonsweet confections if salt and pepper or cheese are added to the dough.

A sweet confection may be made by adding confectioner's sugar to the dough and dusting the finished puff again with the same sugar.

(makes 16 puffs)

1 cake tofu, drained by Method I and liquefied in a blender, food processor, or with an eggbeater	pinch salt
	dash nutmeg
	½ cup sifted all-purpose flour
4 Tbsps butter	3 large eggs

Bring liquefied tofu to a boil in a medium-sized saucepan. Add butter, salt, and nutmeg (add ⅓ cup confectioner's sugar, if making a sweet confection) and wait until butter melts. Reduce heat to very low.

Add flour all at once and stir vigorously with a wooden spoon until mixture forms a compact ball. This should be done over very low heat.

Remove from heat and add eggs one at a time, beating quickly and vigorously until each egg is completely absorbed. This must be done while paste is hot. (Mix in ⅓ cup grated Swiss cheese at this point, if making a savory puff.)

SAMOSA

Here tofu is used as a kind of "cheese" to form a filling for these South Asian delicacies. Compare this to how tofu is used in Piroshki (page 139).

(makes 12 pieces)

dough:
1 cup bread flour
2 Tbsps lard
⅛ tsp cumin seed
⅛ tsp salt
⅓ cup milk

filling:
3 Tbsps butter
1 potato, diced
1 onion, chopped
⅔ cup frozen green peas
1 tomato

¼ tsp each cumin seed, red pepper, black pepper, and cinnamon
1 Tbsp curry powder
1 tsp salt
½ cake "cotton" tofu, drained by Method III and cut into ½-inch cubes
4 ounces cream cheese, cut into ½-inch cubes

4 cups vegetable oil for deep-frying

dough:

In a medium-sized bowl, mix flour, lard, cumin, and salt. Add milk, mix, and knead for 5–6 minutes. Place in plastic wrap and let stand for 30 minutes.

Divide dough into 6 pieces and form each into a ball. Roll out each ball into a 6-inch round. Cut each round in half. Sprinkle each half-round with flour, stack, and cover with plastic wrap.

filling:

Melt butter in frying pan, add potato, onion, green peas, tomato, and spices and sauté over medium heat for 2–3 minutes. Season to taste with salt.

Cover and cook over low heat until potato is soft. Remove lid, raise heat to medium, and cook until liquid evaporates. Remove from heat and add tofu and cream cheese. Mix and cool.

Heat oil to medium-high temperature (350°F).

Divide cooled filling into 12 portions. Place 1 portion of filling in the middle of each half-round of dough. Wet edges of dough with water, then fold over dough to form a triangle with rounded sides, as illustrated.

Place each piece in hot oil as soon as it is folded and deep-fry until light gold.

Eat hot or at room temperature.

PIROSHKI

Tofu is used here instead of the water or milk in yeast breads. Deep-fried piroshki wrapper made in this way is crisp and light, yet a proper yeast dough.

(makes 12 pieces)

dough:
1 ½ tsps dry yeast
¼ tsp sugar
⅓ cup lukewarm water
1 ½ cakes "cotton" tofu, drained by Method I
4 Tbsps butter
1 tsp salt
1 tsp sugar
4 ½ cups all-purpose flour

filling:
4 Tbsps butter

1 lb ground beef
salt and pepper to taste
1 Tbsp flour
1 onion, chopped
2 cloves garlic, chopped
4 cabbage leaves, coarsely chopped and parboiled
1 tsp sugar
2 hard-boiled eggs, chopped
¼ cup finely chopped parsley and dill

vegetable oil for deep-frying

dough:
Mix yeast, sugar, and lukewarm water and let stand until foamy.

Process tofu in blender or food processor until liquid (or use eggbeater or wire whisk).

Melt butter and add salt and sugar. Add liquid tofu to butter and warm over low heat.

Place in large bowl and mix in flour, then yeast.

Knead dough for 5 minutes. Place in oiled bowl, turn once to coat dough with oil, and cover with damp cloth. Let stand in warm place until doubled in bulk—about 1–1 ½ hours.

filling:
Make filling while dough is rising. Melt 2 Tbsps butter, add ground beef, and sauté over medium heat until color turns. Season to taste with salt and pepper. Add 1 Tbsp flour and sauté another 2–3 minutes. Place meat in a large bowl.

Melt 2 Tbsps butter and sauté onion and garlic over medium heat until soft but not golden. Add cabbage and sauté 2–3 minutes. Season with salt, pepper, and sugar.

Add to meat in large bowl. Add hard-boiled egg, chopped parsley, and dill and mix well.

to assemble:
On a lightly floured work surface, roll out dough to ¼-inch thickness. Cut 12 4-inch rounds.

Divide filling into 12 portions.

Generously sprinkle a baking sheet with flour.

Place round of dough on palm of hand. On each round, place 2 generous Tbsps of filling. Fold dough over filling, taking care not to stretch it. Place piroshki folded side down about 2 inches apart on baking sheet.

Sprinkle or spray a little water over piroshki, place in protected, warm place (such as an oven), and let rise until dough expands somewhat—about 40 minutes.

Heat oil to medium temperature (340°F) and deep-fry 2 piroshki at a time, turning constantly, until golden brown.

Best eaten hot, so keep finished piroshki warm in oven while deep-frying remainder.

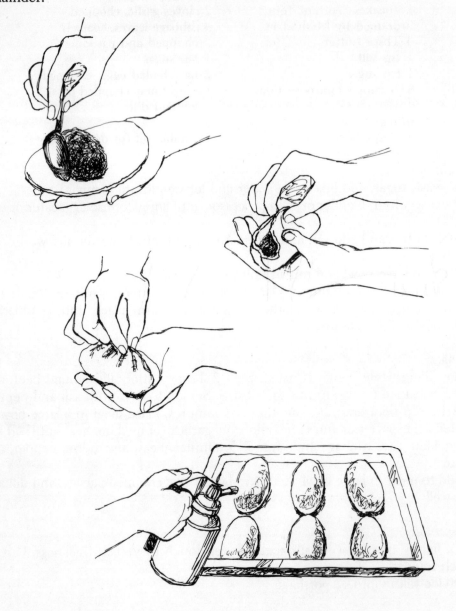

OATMEAL COOKIES

(color plate 23)

Tofu is a marvelous base for cookies. Here is one good example, using an American favorite.

(about 3 dozen, 2-inch cookies)

¼ lb (1 stick) butter, at room temperature
½ cup firmly packed brown sugar
½ cup granulated sugar
½ cake tofu, drained by Method II

1 tsp vanilla extract
1 cup sifted all-purpose flour
½ tsp baking soda
1 tsp baking powder
½ tsp salt
1 cup quick-cooking oats

Preheat oven to 350°F.

Cream butter, then beat in sugars until fluffy. Add tofu and vanilla and beat until smooth. Sift flour, baking soda, baking powder, and salt together and add to the tofu mixture. Mix lightly with rubber spatula, then stir in rolled oats.

Drop 2 inches apart on a well-greased cookie sheet and press lightly with spoon. Bake 10–12 minutes or until light brown.

Variation: Add ½ cup raisins or nuts along with the oats.

RICH WALNUT COOKIES

Everyone will want to know how such rich cookies can be made without butter, eggs, or cream.

(makes 1 ½ dozen)

"A"	"B"
½ cake "cotton" tofu, drained by Method II	1 cup all purpose flour
⅓ cup raw sugar	1 tsp baking powder
2 Tbsps lemon juice	½ tsp salt
	½ cup crushed walnuts
½ cup vegetable oil	1 Tbsp Chinese fermented
⅓ cup sugar	black beans, chopped

Liquefy "A" ingredients in a blender, processor, or with an eggbeater or wire whisk. Place liquid in a heavy enameled skillet or saucepan over low heat and cook, stirring constantly until it thickens. Cool.

Mix oil and sugar in a large bowl. Add tofu mixture and blend.

Sift "B" ingredients together.

Mix "B" into tofu mixture and, when almost blended, add walnuts and fermented black beans.

Heat oven to 400°F.

Form tablespoonfuls of batter into small balls and place 1 inch apart on baking sheet. Press with tines of fork to form flat cookie with corrugated top. Or, just drop tablespoonfuls of batter onto baking sheet.

Bake 10 minutes or until browned. Keeps well, and flavor matures in 2–3 days.

Desserts

FRUIT COMPOTE

"Silk" tofu is the certain "something" that sets this compote apart and makes it a refreshingly original way of serving fruit in season.

(serves 6)

syrup:
1 cup water
1 cup sugar

1 cup champagne or dry white wine
2 Tbsps lemon juice

6 cups fruit in season and/or drained canned fruit, cut into bite-sized pieces
½ cake "silk" tofu, drained by Method I and cut into ½-inch cubes

Boil syrup ingredients until sugar is dissolved, then chill.

Combine syrup, wine, and lemon juice. Add fruit and tofu, mixing carefully because tofu is very fragile. Chill for 1–2 hours before serving.

TOFU ICE CREAM

It was a real challenge to make a delicately flavored sweet that is not dominated by the protein aroma and flavor of tofu. I succeeded; this recipe was successful on the first try, and everyone who has eaten this ice cream is amazed to learn what it is made of. A totally vegetarian variation also was born from this idea.

(makes 3 cups)

1 cake tofu
1 cup heavy cream
½ cup confectioner's sugar
¼ tsp powdered ginger
⅛ tsp nutmeg

1 cup vanilla ice cream
2 Tbsps chopped crystalliz-ed ginger

Blend tofu, cream, sugar, powdered ginger, and nutmeg in blender or food processor, or with an eggbeater.

Place in container or covered bowl and freeze for 3 hours or until ice crystals begin to form. Mix well with a wire whisk. Repeat this process twice more.

Blend in vanilla ice cream and crystallized ginger and freeze again.

Vegetarian variation: Walnut-Tofu Ice "Cream"
Simmer ½ cup walnuts and 1 cup water for 10 minutes over low heat.

Place walnuts and boiling water in blender or food processor and blend until as smooth as possible. Strain through a sieve.

Substitute this walnut cream for heavy cream in the basic recipe and add 1 tsp vanilla extract. Proceed as in basic recipe, omitting the vanilla ice cream.

BANANA CUSTARD

(color plate 23)

This is hardly an exotic or startlingly new recipe, but it does demonstrate the virtues of soy milk. This custard is lighter and has a deeper flavor than one made with cow's milk.

(serves 4)

custard cream:
1 ½ cups soy milk
3 egg yolks
½ cup sugar
¼ cup flour
¼ cup heavy cream

1 Tbsp butter
½ tsp vanilla extract
1 Tbsp rum
4 bananas, cut into ¼-inch
    slices

Warm the soy milk in a saucepan but do not let it boil. Beat egg yolks and sugar. Sift in flour, blend, then add warm soy milk a little at a time. Cook in a double boiler, stirring constantly, for 10–15 minutes or until very smooth and glossy. Remove from heat and stir in heavy cream, butter, vanilla extract, and rum. While the custard is still hot, mix in banana slices. Serve chilled.

EASY CHEESECAKE

cheesecake:
8 ounces cream cheese
1 cup sour cream
1/3–1/2 cup confectioner's
    sugar
1/2 tsp nutmeg
1/2 cake tofu, drained by
    Method II

topping:
1/2 cup red currant jelly
2–3 Tbsps sugar
1/4 cup lemon juice
3 lbs strawberries, washed,
    patted dry, and crushed
1/4 cup kirsch

1/4 cup chopped walnuts

Combine all cheesecake ingredients in a blender or food processor and process until creamy. Fold in walnuts.

Line a 2-quart mold of any shape with cheesecloth. Pour in cheese-tofu mixture and cover with cheesecloth. Cover with flat lid, weight lightly, and refrigerate for not less than 3–4 hours, but preferably overnight.

Remove from mold, remove cheesecloth, and serve on a decorative plate with strawberry topping in a separate bowl.

strawberry topping:
Simmer red currant jelly, sugar, and lemon juice until sugar dissolves. Cool. Add strawberries and kirsch and refrigerate 1–2 hours.

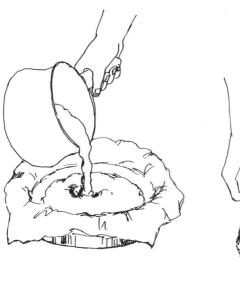

BLUEBERRY-CHEESE PIE

(10-inch pie)

pastry:
1 ½ cups all-purpose flour
½ tsp salt
6 Tbsps butter
1 Tbsp shortening
3–4 Tbsps cold water

filling:
4 ounces cream cheese, at
   room temperature
½ cake tofu, drained by
   Method I
⅓ cup sugar
2 large eggs
6 Tbsps sweet butter
⅛ tsp nutmeg
2 tsps vanilla extract

topping:
2 Tbsps gelatin
2 Tbsps cold water
⅓ cup apricot jam
3 Tbsps lemon juice
12-ounce can blueberries,
   drained

pastry:
Mix flour and salt in medium-sized bowl. Cut in butter and shortening until mixture resembles coarse crumbs. Gradually mix in water with fingers until mixture leaves sides of bowl. Gather into a ball and flatten slightly. Wrap in plastic wrap and refrigerate for 1 hour.

Preheat oven to 375°F.

Roll pastry on lightly floured surface into 12-inch circle about ⅛-inch thick. Line 10-inch pie plate and trim flush with edge. Line pastry with aluminum foil and weight with a smaller pie plate. Bake until pastry is set—about 10 minutes. Remove foil and cool to room temperature. Reduce oven temperature to 325°F for filling.

filling:
Cream all ingredients in blender or processor until smooth, about 2–3 minutes. Pour filling into pie shell and bake for 35 minutes. Cool.

topping:
Soften gelatin in water. Heat apricot jam and lemon juice until jam has melted. Remove from heat and stir in soaked gelatin until completely dissolved. Add blueberries and cool. Pour blueberry mixture over the cheese filling and chill.

COTTAGE CHEESE PIE

Tofu can look deceptively like cottage cheese when drained and mashed. Used in a half-and-half combination with cottage cheese, it will impart a lightness difficult to achieve using cheese alone. I use it a lot in my cheese-based desserts for this very reason.

(9-inch pie)

pastry:
1 ½ cups all-purpose flour
¼ cup sugar
¼ tsp salt
6 Tbsps butter
2 Tbsps shortening
1 egg yolk
2 Tbsps ice water

filling:
12 ounces small curd cottage cheese
½ cake tofu, drained by Method II, patted dry, and mashed
½ cup sugar

3 Tbsps butter, at room temperature
½ cup sifted flour
3 egg yolks
2 drops almond extract
1 tsp vanilla extract
½ tsp salt
¼ cup raisins, dredged with flour
1 Tbsp each finely chopped orange peel and lemon peel, dredged with flour

glaze:
1 egg yolk
2 Tbsps water

pastry:
Combine flour, sugar, salt, butter, and shortening and work ingredients together quickly with fingertips until mixture resembles coarse meal. Stir in egg yolk and water and gather into a ball. Wrap in plastic wrap and refrigerate for 1 hour.

Preheat oven to 375°F.

Roll out ¾ of the dough and line a 9-inch springform pan. Line pastry with aluminum foil and weight with another pan, beans, etc. Bake 10 minutes and cool. Roll out the remaining dough in a 10-inch circle ⅛-inch thick for top crust. Refrigerate.

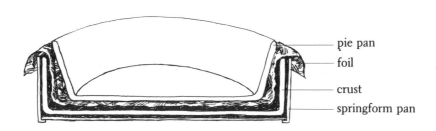

pie pan
foil
crust
springform pan

filling:
Place cottage cheese and tofu in a processor or blender and process until smooth. Add sugar, butter, flour, egg yolks, almond extract, vanilla, and salt and process for an additional 2–3 minutes or until a butterlike paste is obtained. Add raisins and peel, mix well, and pour into the pie shell.

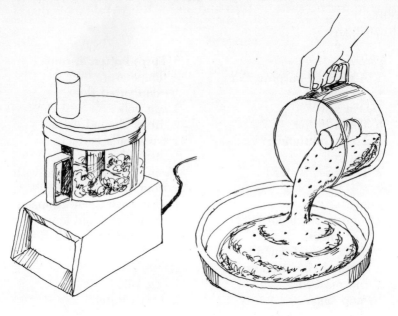

Combine egg yolk and water and brush onto rim of bottom pie crust. Cover with top crust and press firmly around edge. Brush top crust with glaze. Cut 3–4 steam vents in top crust and bake for 50–60 minutes at 375°F.

PUMPKIN PIE
(color plate 23)

Tofu can be used in two ways in pumpkin pie. This recipe highlights the qualities of "silk" tofu, which contrast with the spicy flavor and texture of the pie. The other way is to mash "cotton" tofu and add it to the pumpkin filling.

(10-inch pie)

pastry:
1 ½ cups all-purpose flour
¼ tsp salt
4 Tbsps butter
4 Tbsps lard
4–5 Tbsps ice water

1 Tbsp sesame seeds

½ cake "silk" tofu, diced
   and marinated overnight
   in the apple juice and 1
   tsp fresh ginger juice

filling:
2 cups fresh or canned
   pumkin puree
½ cup each milk and heavy cream
½ cup sugar
3 egg yolks
¼ cup molasses or raw sugar
1 Tbsp cinnamon
¼ tsp each powdered ginger
   and cloves
4 Tbsps melted butter
¼ cup apple juice or cider

3 egg whites
pinch salt

pastry:
Mix flour, salt, butter, and lard with fingertips (or pastry blender or food processor) until the consistency of cornmeal. Add cold water and mix until the dough is smooth, working as quickly as possible.

Roll out the dough and line 10-inch pie pan. Sprinkle with sesame seeds.

Preheat oven to 375°F.

Remove tofu from apple juice.

Place all the filling ingredients (including apple juice) in a food processor or blender and process until smooth.

Beat the egg whites and salt until very stiff. Mix half of the egg whites and all of the pumpkin filling together with a rubber spatula. Fold in the rest of the egg whites and pour half the filling into the pie shell. Sprinkle tofu cubes over filling, then add remaining pumpkin.

Bake for 50 minutes or until filling is firm and surface is slightly dry.

Cool to room temperature and serve with vanilla ice cream or creme chantilly.

filling
tofu
filling

SPICE CAKE

Here tofu enriches the texture and flavor of this elegant spice cake. Using tofu sautéed until a firm curd was formed was a gamble that paid off handsomely.

(9-inch loaf)

"A"
2 1/3 cups cake flour
2 tsps baking powder
1/2 tsp salt

"B"
3/4 cup butter, at room temperature
1 1/3 cups sugar (or 1 cup granulated and 1/3 cup brown sugar)
4 egg yolks
1 tsp each nutmeg, cinnamon, cardamom, and allspice
1/2 tsp each mace, powdered ginger, and cloves

1/2 cup cottage cheese
1/2 cake "cotton" tofu, drained by Method III and sautéed for 10 minutes without oil, until it resembles cottage cheese

4 egg whites
pinch salt

icing:
1/3 cup loose brown sugar
2 Tbsps lemon juice

topping:
3 Tbsps poppy seeds

Preheat oven to 350°F.

Mix "A" ingredients and sift twice.

Cream butter and sugar, then blend in egg yolks 1 at a time. Mix in spices, then cottage cheese and sautéed tofu.

Beat egg whites with a pinch salt until stiff but not dry.

Sift "A" into "B" gradually, mixing as you do so.

Fold beaten egg white into batter.

Pour into buttered 9-inch loaf pan and bake 30 minutes or until a skewer comes out clean.

While cake is baking, mix brown sugar and lemon juice. Spread on hot cake and sprinkle with poppy seeds.

Return cake to oven for 10 minutes.

Leave cake in pan for 5–10 minutes after removing from oven, then remove from pan and cool on rack.

ELEGANT BREAD PUDDING

This is an aristocratic bread pudding made transcendent by tofu and a sophisticated, rich sauce of bourbon whiskey.

²/₃ cup raisins
¹/₃ cup bourbon whiskey
2 cups milk
¹/₂ cake tofu, pureed
5–6 cups French bread cut
    into 1-inch cubes
3 medium eggs, beaten
¹/₂ cup sugar
6 Tbsps melted butter
2 tsps vanilla extract
1 tsp cinnamon

whiskey sauce:
¹/₄ cup water
6 Tbsps butter
¹/₃ cup sugar
2 medium eggs, well beaten
¹/₄ cup bourbon whiskey

Soak raisins in whiskey overnight or until plump.

Mix milk and pureed tofu well and pour over French bread cubes. Let stand about ¹/₂ hour, until absorbed by bread.

Preheat oven to 375°F.

Mix eggs and sugar until sugar is totally dissolved. Blend in melted butter and vanilla. Pour this mixture over French bread and mix well. Mix in raisins (including any remaining whiskey).

Butter a 3-quart soufflé dish and pour in pudding mixture. Sprinkle with cinnamon.

Place soufflé dish in a large baking pan containing 1 inch boiling water and bake for 1 hour, until the top is browned.

While pudding is baking, make whiskey sauce. Simmer water, butter, and sugar over low heat. Combine beaten egg and whiskey and add to simmering mixture 1 Tbsp at a time while beating liquid with a wire whisk. Take care that the heat is not too high, or the egg will harden.

Serve pudding hot with hot whiskey sauce.

CHINESE TOFU CUSTARD
(color plate 24)

This dessert is a children's favorite in Taiwan, where it is still sold by street vendors. So simple to make, it is wonderfully refreshing and, if topped with dates (dried jujubes are used in China), takes on an authentic Chinese flavor.

(serves 4)

1 cake tofu, drained by
    Method II and mashed (2
    cups)
½ cup honey

1 drop almond extract
1 tsp lemon juice
4 dates (or "red dates"), cut
    in half

Mix tofu, honey, almond extract, and lemon juice well and chill. Serve topped with dates.

YUBA ROLLS WITH SWEET BEAN JAM
(color plate 25)

Yuba is the skin that forms when soy milk is boiled. In its dried form it keeps almost indefinitely, but is quite brittle. It comes packaged in small sheets.

(about 12 rolls)

vegetable oil for deep-frying
dried *yuba* sheets, cut into
    3-inch squares with
    scissors

8-ounce can sweet azuki
    bean paste (*anko*), either
    chunky or pureed

Heat oil to low temperature (320°F).

Reconstitute *yuba* by spraying squares with a fine mist of water or immersing in warm water briefly then spreading on a kitchen towel. Place 1 ½ Tbsps sweet bean paste in the center of each square and fold as illustrated, wetting edges and pressing so that the roll will not loosen. Deep-fry, turning often, until golden, about 7–8 minutes. Drain on paper towels. Sprinkle with a very small amount of salt. Serve hot or at room temperature.

Index

VEGETARIAN DISHES